DATE DUE

MODERN WORLD CULTURES

Africa South of the Sahara

Australia and the Pacific

East Asia

Europe

Latin America

North Africa and the Middle East

Northern America

Russia and
the Former Soviet Republics

South Asia

Southeast Asia

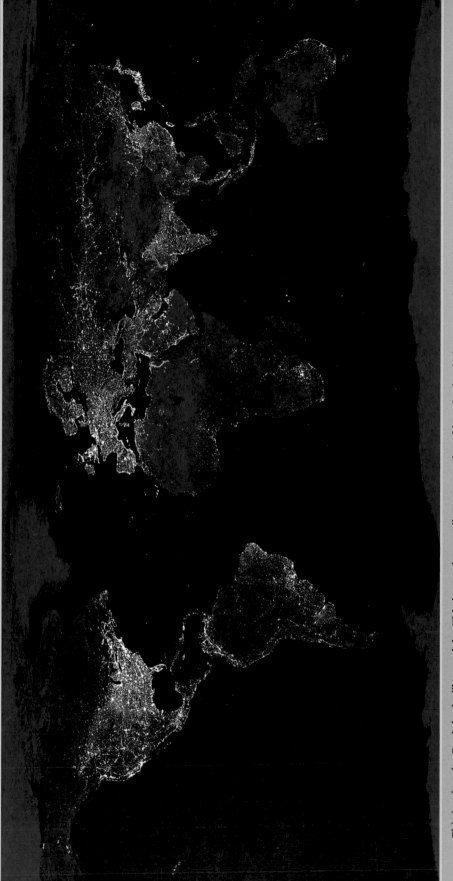

This is what the Earth looks like at night. This image is actually a composite of hundreds of pictures made by orbiting satellites. Man-made lights highlight the developed or populated areas of the Earth's surface. The dark areas include the central part of South America, Africa, Asia, and Australia.

(Credit: C. Mayhew and R. Simmon; NASA/GSFC, NOAA/NGDC, DMSP Digital Archive.)

Southeast Asia

Douglas A. Phillips
Senior Consultant
Center for Civic Education
Calabasas, CA

Series Consulting Editor
Charles F. Gritzner
South Dakota State University

CHELSEA HOUSE
PUBLISHERS
A Haights Cross Communications ✈ Company ®
Philadelphia

Cover: Fishing boats in Hon Gai Harbor, Vietnam

CHELSEA HOUSE PUBLISHERS

VP, NEW PRODUCT DEVELOPMENT Sally Cheney
DIRECTOR OF PRODUCTION Kim Shinners
CREATIVE MANAGER Takeshi Takahashi
MANUFACTURING MANAGER Diann Grasse
PRODUCTION EDITOR Noelle Nardone
PHOTO EDITOR Sarah Bloom

Staff for SOUTHEAST ASIA

EXECUTIVE EDITOR Lee M. Marcott
EDITORIAL ASSISTANT Joseph Gialanella
DEVELOPMENTAL EDITOR Carol Field
PROJECT MANAGER Michael Henry
SERIES AND COVER DESIGNER Takeshi Takahashi
LAYOUT Maryland Composition Company, Inc.

A Haights Cross Communications ✈ Company ®

http://www.chelseahouse.com

First Printing

10 9 8 7 6 5 4 3 2 1

Library of Congress Cataloging-in-Publication Data

Phillips, Douglas A.
  Southeast Asia / Douglas A. Phillips.
      p. cm. — (Modern world cultures)
  Includes bibliographical references and index.
  ISBN 0-7910-8149-4 (hard cover)
  1. Asia, Southeastern—Juvenile literature. I. Title. II. Series.
  DS521.P47 2005
  959—dc22

                                        2005010043

TABLE OF CONTENTS

Charles F. Gritzner

Geography is the key that unlocks the door to the world's won-ders. There are, of course, many ways of viewing the world and its diverse physical and human features. In this series—MODERN WORLD CULTURES—the emphasis is on people and their cultures. As you step through the geographic door into the ten world cultures covered in this series, you will come to better know, understand, and appreciate the world's mosaic of peoples and how they live. You will see how different peoples adapt to, use, and change their natural environments. And you will be amazed at the vast differences in thinking, doing, and living practiced around the world. The MODERN WORLD CULTURES series was developed in response to many requests from librarians and teachers throughout the United States and Canada.

As you begin your reading tour of the world's major cultures, it is important that you understand three terms that are used throughout the series: geography, culture, and region. These words and their meanings are often misunderstood. **Geography** is an age-old way of viewing the varied features of Earth's surface. In fact, it is the oldest of the existing sciences! People have *always* had a need to know about and understand their surroundings. In times past, a people's world was their immediate surroundings; today, our world is global in scope. Events occuring half a world away can and often do have an immediate impact on our lives. If we, either individually or as a nation of peoples, are to be successful in the global community, it is essential that we know and understand our neighbors, regardless of who they are or where they may live.

Geography and history are similar in many ways; both are methodologies—distinct ways of viewing things and events. Historians are concerned with time, or when events happened. Geographers, on the other hand, are concerned with space, or where things are located. In essence, geographers ask: "What is where, why there, and why care?" in regard to various physical and human features of Earth's surface.

Culture has many definitions. For this series and for most geographers and anthropologists, it refers to a people's *way of life*. This means the totality of everything we possess because we are human, such as our ideas, beliefs, and customs, including language, religious beliefs, and all knowledge. Tools and skills also are an important aspect of culture. Different cultures, after all, have different types of technology and levels of technological attainment that they can use in performing various tasks. Finally, culture includes social interactions—the ways different people interact with one another individually and as groups.

Finally, the idea of **region** is one geographers use to organize and analyze geographic information spatially. A region is an area that is set apart from others on the basis of one or more unifying elements. Language, religion, and major types of economic activity are traits that often are used by geographers to separate one region from another. Most geographers, for example, see a cultural division between Northern, or Anglo, America and Latin America. That "line" is usually drawn at the U.S.-Mexico boundary, although there is a broad area of transition and no actual cultural line exists.

The ten culture regions presented in this series have been selected on the basis of their individuality, or uniqueness. As you tour the world's culture realms, you will learn something of their natural environment, history, and way of living. You will also learn about their population and settlement, how they govern themselves, and how they make their living. Finally, you will take a peek into the future in the hope of identifying each region's challenges and prospects. Enjoy your trip!

Charles F. ("Fritz") Gritzner
Department of Geography
South Dakota State University
May 2005

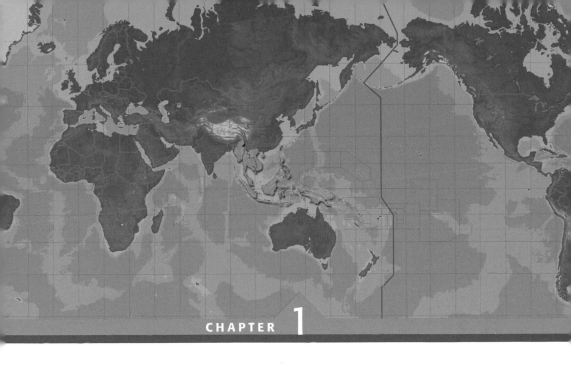

CHAPTER 1

Getting Acquainted
With Southeast Asia

Southeast Asia brings to mind exotic people and exotic places that seem very far away. From the beautiful beaches of Bali, Indonesia, to the bustling modern city of Singapore, this region is home to many ancient cultures that are developing modern political structures and economies. This transition is taking many of the people of Southeast Asia on a whirlwind ride. They are moving from an era of European colonial economies built on the lucrative spice trade to twenty-first-century technical jobs created in the age of computers, biotechnology, and the Internet.

Politically, Southeast Asia is made up of ten countries. Indonesia, Singapore, the Philippines, and Brunei Darussalam (Brunei) are island nations. Burma (also called Myanmar), Thailand, Cambodia

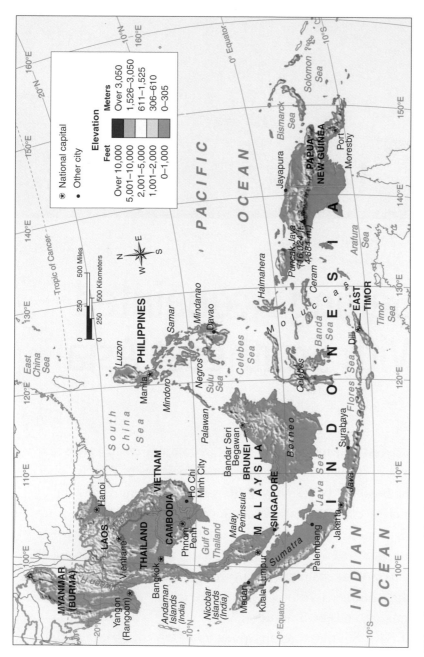

This reference map of Southeast Asia shows the countries, cities, and elevations of the ten countries and many islands that make up this region of the world. The countries of this region stretch across vast expanses of land and water.

Fishing boats rest at the shore of Bali, Indonesia. Made up of nearly 17,000 islands (6,000 inhabited), Indonesia relies on the water not only for fishing but also for travel, trade, and communication.

(also called Kampuchea), Laos, and Vietnam are countries of the Southeast Asian mainland. Malaysia includes the mainland's Malay Peninsula and the island of Borneo. These countries stretch across vast expanses of land and water, spanning a distance of 3,500 miles (5,600 kilometers) from Burma in the west to West Papua (Irian Jaya) in Indonesia. The region spans approximately 18 degrees of latitude (1,250 miles, or 2,000 kilometers) north to south. Burma reaches farthest to the north in the region, and sprawling Indonesia is Southeast Asia's southernmost country. Nearly all of Southeast Asia is located within the tropics. The equator passes through Indonesia, leaving roughly half of its territory in the Southern Hemisphere.

Southeast Asia

Southeast Asia is divided by political boundaries established by both land and water. Thus, the region includes land borders with Bangladesh and India in the west and China in the north. From there, the Luzon Strait and the Philippine Sea serve as water boundaries on the north and northeast and the Pacific Ocean borders the region on the east. The area splits the island of New Guinea, including only the Indonesian portion of the island. (Culturally, the eastern half of the island of New Guinea is a part of the region that includes Australia, New Zealand, and the Pacific.) To the south, the Arafura and Timor seas connect the Pacific Ocean to the Indian Ocean, which borders Southeast Asia on the west and southwest.

Some of the countries in this region are fragmented, scattered over thousands of islands. The Philippines is an archipelago (chain of islands) of more than 7,000 islands located 500 miles (800 kilometers) off the coast of Southeast Asia. Although the Philippines create an impressive archipelago, it is relatively small when compared to the world's largest island chain. Nearly 17,000 islands—6,000 are inhabited—form the country of Indonesia. The vast number of islands creates many problems. Governing a spatially fragmented country is difficult, and, because of the extreme remoteness of some areas, so are travel, trade, and communication.

Southeast Asia has been and continues to be a strategic region, in part because of some of the narrow waterways that exist in key locations. The Strait of Malacca has been of great historical importance as nations have struggled to control this key passage. Piracy has existed in the region for centuries and continues today with frequent attacks in the waters around Indonesia and Vietnam. This again demonstrates the importance and fragility of the water "highways" in this region. They are vital in keeping the global flow of trade in oil, manufactured goods, and other resources moving.

The following chart introduces the countries of Southeast Asia and provides basic information about each.

COUNTRIES OF SOUTHEAST ASIA

	Official Country Name	Capital	Population	Land Area in Square Miles (Square Kilometers)	Coastline in Miles (Kilometers)	Bordering Countries
Brunei	Negara Brunei Darussalam	Bandar Seri Begawan	358,098	2,228 (5,770)	100 (161)	Malaysia
Burma*	Union of Burma	Yangon	42,510,537	261,969 (678,500)	1,200 (1,930)	China, India, Laos, Bangladesh, Thailand
Cambodia	Kingdom of Cambodia	Phnom Penh	13,124,764	69,900 (181,040)	275 (443)	Thailand, Vietnam, Laos
Indonesia	Republic of Indonesia	Jakarta	234,893,453	741,097 (1,919,440)	34,006 (54,716)	Papua New Guinea, Malaysia
Laos	Lao People's Democratic Republic	Vientiane	5,921,545	91,429 (236,800)	None	Burma, China, Cambodia, Thailand, Vietnam
Malaysia	Malaysia	Kuala Lumpur	23,092,940	127,217 (329,750)	2,905 (4,675)	Brunei, Indonesia, Thailand
Philippines	Republic of the Philippines	Manila	84,619,974	115,830 (300,000)	22,554 (36,289)	None
Singapore	Republic of Singapore	Singapore	4,608,595	267 (692.7)	120 (193)	None (connected to Malaysia by a causeway)
Thailand	Kingdom of Thailand	Bangkok	64,265,276	198,456 (514,000)	2,001 (3,219)	Burma, Laos, Cambodia, Malaysia
Vietnam	Socialist Republic of Viet Nam	Hanoi	81,624,716	127,243 (329,560)	2,140 (3,444)	Cambodia, China, Laos

* The term *Burma* is used in this book because the United States and many other countries do not recognize the name *Myanmar*, which was imposed by the military government.

Southeast Asia covers approximately 1.75 million square miles (4.5 million square kilometers), roughly half the area of the 48 continental United States. Countries range in size from Indonesia, with a land area about three times the size of Texas, to tiny Singapore, which is only about three and a half times the size of Washington, D.C. Countries with easy access to the sea because of vast coastlines like those of Indonesia and the Philippines contrast sharply with landlocked Laos. In terms of population, Indonesia is the most populated, with more than 230 million people. Sparsely populated Brunei has fewer than 500,000 people.

The personality of the land is both tranquil and volatile—perhaps more so than any other area in the world. It can be a tropical paradise, with lush forests, beautiful beaches, and clear tropical waters. As the world has learned on numerous occasions, however, this can also be one of Earth's most treacherous regions. Much of Southeast Asia lies astride the Ring of Fire, a zone known for earthquakes and volcanoes that surrounds the Pacific Ocean basin. Violent volcanic eruptions include those of Mount Tambora, Krakatau (also called Krakatoa), and Mount Pinatubo. On December 26, 2004, one of the most violent earthquakes ever recorded struck a short distance off the northwest coast of Sumatra, an island of Indonesia. The resulting tsunami (seismic sea wave) killed an estimated 250,000 people in areas as distant as the east coast of Africa.

Political tension in the region can be as violent as the natural environment. Historically, Southeast Asia is a region of unrest. Some problems were civil conflicts among two or more of the region's many ethnic or religious groups. Over the past 500 years, various European powers have been involved in numerous military disputes. The region also was the site of a major conflict during the 1960s. In the Vietnamese Conflict, nearly 60,000 U.S. military personnel lost their lives.

Today, terrorists pose the major threat to human life and property. In 2002, a bomb killed more than 200 people, mostly tourists, in Bali, Indonesia. An al Qaeda–affiliated group based in Southeast Asia claimed responsibility for the attack. The event demonstrated the worldwide reach that modern terrorists possess. During the summer of 2003, a popular hotel in Jakarta, Indonesia, was bombed. It, too, was an attempt by the same group—Jemaah Islamiyah—to disrupt the region politically and economically. Even Christians have been involved in terrorism. A Christian group is believed to have been responsible for the bombing of a large Muslim mosque in Jakarta in 1999.

Political volatility is not always associated with religious groups. There are also separatist groups that operate in Southeast Asian countries such as Indonesia, Thailand, and the Philippines. The greatest growing threat, however, seems to be coming from additional violent Islamic groups, including the Gerakan Mujahidin Islam Pattani in Thailand and Abu Sayyaf in the Philippines. Both of these groups are believed to have close ties to al Qaeda.

The physical and political environments are volatile, but this does not necessarily forecast a fear-filled future for the region. The problems that relate to regional political instability seem to be declining; in fact, throughout much of the region, democracy appears to be getting stronger. Indonesia, Singapore, Malaysia, Thailand, and the Philippines are strengthening democratic practices. Elsewhere, countries such as Laos, Cambodia, and Vietnam are moving away from Communist practices. Burma has become somewhat isolated in the international community because of its antidemocratic practices and military rule. International pressure seems to be moving Burma slowly toward a more inclusive political process, and Brunei, a monarchy, also seems to be considering more democratic practices.

Economic activity directly connects Southeast Asia to the rest of the world. Singapore, Indonesia, Malaysia, Thailand, and the Philippines are all active trading nations. Their goods find their way to one another's markets and also to those in Western countries. Products manufactured in this region range from clothing and toys to high-tech computer chips, laptop computers, and circuit boards. Intel, Samsung, Toshiba, and other leading companies have a strong industrial presence in Southeast Asia. They are attracted by a skilled work force combined with reasonable wages.

The Association of Southeast Asian Nations (ASEAN) has helped propel this region rapidly forward since it was founded in 1967. All ten Southeast Asian countries are now members; Cambodia, the last to join, became a member in 1999. The thrust of this organization is primarily economic, but it also has interests in social and cultural development and in promoting political stability in the region and partner countries. The successes of ASEAN are great, and the economic and political influence of the group on the international scene has been tremendous.

The people of Southeast Asia present a wonderful mosaic of humanity. The major religions of the world are present, along with a huge array of languages. Graceful dances and music provide glimpses of the traditional cultures. Today, however, they are often punctuated with the liveliness and fast pace of modern music. Increasingly, this once-traditional area now draws not only from its own culture but also from the popular culture of the West. This means that a movie from the West may be shown in a theater next door to a popular movie that was made in India's Bollywood. This mix of East and West, traditional and modern, gives Southeast Asian countries a vibrance and feeling of excitement that makes travel in the region very enticing.

Today, the people of Southeast Asia have become the neighbors and friends of others in Western and Eastern societies. During the past half-century, many people have moved from the region to places around the world. Canada, many European countries, Australia, the United States, and others have taken in thousands of immigrants from Southeast Asia who have brought their culture and economic savvy to their new homes. This has helped further economic development

Pictured here are children of Cambodia. One of many diverse cultures found in Southeast Asia, Cambodia was the last to join the Association of Southeast Asian Nations (ASEAN) in 1999.

within the region and has added greatly to the cultural diversity in the West.

Today, the importance of the Southeast Asian culture realm is ever present. It may be found in the shrimp you eat, the clothes you wear, the computer you use, or the ancestry of a close friend. This book examines in greater detail the past, present, and potential of this region, along with the connections the region has with the rest of the world. May your visit to this fascinating culture realm be both enjoyable and informative!

CHAPTER 2

Nature

On December 26, 2004, a gigantic earthquake—the strongest recorded in 40 years—struck the floor of the Indian Ocean just off of the northwest coast of the Indonesian island of Sumatra. The resulting tsunami swept across the Indian Ocean basin, bringing death and destruction to people in 11 countries, some as far away as East Africa. United Nations estimates place the death toll at nearly 250,000. In addition, at least half a million people were injured and millions more were left homeless. Within months, more than 4 billion dollars in aid had been pledged by donors from countries all over the world. Hardest hit were low-lying islands, coastal fishing villages, and tourist centers such as Phuket, Thailand. As millions of people went about their daily tasks or basked on the beach enjoying

Vast areas of destruction were left behind by a devastating tsunami in Banda Aceh, Indonesia. Damage from the December 26, 2004, tsunami was seen as far away as East Africa.

a vacation, a huge wall of water—more than 20 feet (6 meters) high in some places—crashed ashore. The surging water swept all in its wake inland and then back out to sea. Never in history has an environmental disaster affected as huge an area.

This tragic event spotlights many elements of humankind's relationship to the natural environment of Southeast Asia. First, it is one of the most volatile regions on Earth. The region's history is marked by numerous violent volcanic eruptions, destructive earthquakes, huge tsunamis, and devastating floods. Second, it is a region where many people live very close to land and sea, depending on both for their livelihood. Fishing villages dot the coasts, and farmers are drawn to the fertile alluvial (stream-deposited) soils of the low-lying coastal plains. Third, Southeast Asia is a region dominated by peninsulas and islands, giving maximum exposure to the sea and its occasional wrath. Finally, the region's warm tropical climate, spectacular scenery, and vast expanses of sandy beaches backed by swaying palms create a tourist paradise.

This chapter provides a closer look at the ways in which people in Southeast Asia have adapted to, used, and changed the natural environments in which they live.

ISOLATION AND CULTURE

Through time, semi-isolation from other regions has helped the people of Southeast Asia develop a culture unlike any other. Cultural diffusion—ideas, materials, and even people coming from elsewhere—is the primary cause of culture change. If an area is difficult to reach, its people (and therefore their culture) may be less affected by outside influences.

Southwest Asia stretches 4,000 miles (6,400 kilometers) east–west from Burma to central New Guinea. Its north–south extent, from southern Indonesia to northern Burma, is about 2,500 miles (4,000 kilometers). Superimposed over the United States, northern Burma would lie in southeastern Alaska, the southern islands of Indonesia would span an area from California to Florida, and most of New Guinea would be in the Atlantic Ocean off the coast of the Carolinas. Within this vast expanse, however, is only about 1.8 million square miles (4.6 million square kilometers) of land—an area roughly the size of the continental United States west of the Mississippi River.

Several factors contribute to the region's isolation. To the west, tropical highlands and steaming rain forests have long served as a barrier that isolates the culture realm from the Indian "subcontinent." High plateaus and rugged mountains form a towering barrier between the region and China. Throughout history, water itself was a formidable barrier: The oceanic portion of the realm is composed of tens of thousands of scattered islands. Even today, many islands remain remote, unsettled, and largely untouched.

LAND FEATURES

Fertile river valleys, coastal plains, and rugged terrain formed by mountains, plateaus, and hills dominate the physical landscape of Southeast Asia. On the mainland, a series of rivers that flow southward from their headwaters in China create broad floodplains. The plains and associated fertile soils of the Irrawaddy, Salween, Mekong, and Red rivers support huge population densities. Rice, the major crop, is grown in flooded fields that characterize the region's rural landscape.

Indonesia (17,000 islands) and the Philippines (7,000 islands) are archipelagos. Both countries have rough terrain and areas of fertile plains where most people live and farm. Seven of Indonesia's islands have mountain peaks that reach higher than 10,000 feet (3,050 meters). On New Guinea, the glacier-crowned crest of Puncak Jaya towers 16,503 feet (5,030 meters) above the tropical coastal plain below. Most of peninsular Southeast Asia is quite stable geologically—that is, there are few volcanoes and earthquakes are rare, although they do occur.

A Treacherous Land

Geologically, Indonesia and the Philippines lie astride one of the world's most active and hazardous zones—the Ring of Fire along the Pacific Ocean basin. Here, huge tectonic plates (pieces of Earth's crust) grind against each other, creating zones of frequent volcanic and seismic (earthquake) activity. On the Ring of Fire, mountains that belch ash, fiery clouds of hot volcanic gases and smoke, and glowing lava are not uncommon. Each year, Southeast Asia experiences hundreds of earthquakes, an average of about 500 in Indonesia alone. Underwater volcanic explosions and seismic activity often cause treacherous tsunamis (incorrectly called "tidal waves"), which can devastate low-lying coastal regions.

In Indonesia alone, an estimated 400 volcanoes remain active and 70 eruptions have occurred since 1600. Since A.D. 1000, 23 volcanic disasters have resulted in more than 1,000 deaths.

Ash clouds from Mount Pinatubo, background, hang over an abandoned native hut in Zambales, about 55 miles (89 kilometers) northwest of Manila, Philippines. Volcanic activity began on Mount Pinatubo on June 9, 1991, for the first time in 600 years, spewing ash-laden steam clouds for 8 hours.

Nine of these occurred in Indonesia and two in the Philippines. In 2001, Mount Pinatubo, on the island of Luzon in the Philippines, erupted, resulting in the loss of 800 lives. The eruption also discharged huge amounts of greenhouse gases and volcanic ash into the upper atmosphere. Meteorologists (scientists who study weather) estimate that, for several years, Northern Hemisphere summers were up to 4°F (2°C) cooler and winters were up to 6°F (3°C) colder.

Two of History's Greatest Volcanic Eruptions
Mount Tambora
Indonesia has experienced two of recorded history's most explosive volcanic eruptions. In 1815, on Sumbawa Island, located 200 miles (320 kilometers) east of Java, Mount Tambora exploded in a violent eruption. The death toll will never be known, but it is estimated that 12,000 people lost their lives as a direct result of the explosion. Another 80,000 are believed to have died as a result of starvation, because much agricultural land lay buried beneath a blanket of volcanic ash. Ash and gases from the eruption were thrust into the upper atmosphere, reducing sunlight for several years. Because of the atmospheric blanket, Earth's temperatures dropped by about 5°F (3°C), causing 1816 to be called the "the year without a summer."

Krakatau
The 1883 eruption of Krakatau (Krakatoa) was not as catastrophic as that of Tambora in terms of loss of life, but it is much better documented. It is also better known, thanks to a geographically incorrect 1969 film entitled *Krakatoa, East of Java*. The volcano actually is west of Java in the Sunda Strait. The eruption occurred on August 26, 1883. On Rodriguez Island, located off the coast of Madagascar in the western Indian Ocean, residents heard a rumbling sound much like distant thunder. What they were hearing was the sound of Krakatau's violent eruption that had happened nearly 3,000 miles (4,800 kilometers) away.

A recent book by Thomas Simkin and Richard Fiske, *Krakatoa: The Day the World Exploded,* documented what certainly was one of the most violent geologic events in history. The explosion blew rock debris up to 17 miles (23 kilometers) into the atmosphere. Two-thirds of the island was blown away, and where land once had been, the water was up to 1,000 feet (300 meters) deep. The resulting giant tsunami sent waves up to 120 feet (40 meters) tall crashing into nearby coasts. In some places, the huge wall of water pushed 6 miles (9.5 kilometers) inland, sweeping away everything in its path. The final toll of destruction will never be known. It is believed that 165 coastal villages were destroyed and an estimated 36,000 to 37,000 lives were lost. Gases and volcanic ash in the atmosphere created vibrant sunrises and sunsets for three years. During the year after the eruption, temperatures dropped about 2°F (1°C), and they were cooler than average for five years.

WEATHER AND CLIMATE

Southeast Asia falls within three climatic zones, all of which are tropical or subtropical. Throughout the region, temperatures are mild. Crops can be grown all year, livestock do not need sheltering, and humans have little need to adapt to cold. Moisture is adequate: Almost the entire region receives more than 40 inches (100 centimeters) of rain. Both temperature and precipitation are influenced by three primary controls: latitudinal location, the sea, and elevation.

Indonesia, the Philippines, and coastal regions of the peninsular mainland have a hot, humid, tropical climate. Day after day, the weather is nearly the same—monotonously boring! It is often said that "nighttime is the 'winter' of the tropics." Differences between nighttime and daytime temperature range from the low 70s to low 90s Fahrenheit (25° to 32°C). Surprisingly, perhaps, temperatures rarely, if ever, reach 100°F (38°C). Seasonal temperatures change by only a few degrees. In most of the tropical region, the difference between coldest and warmest

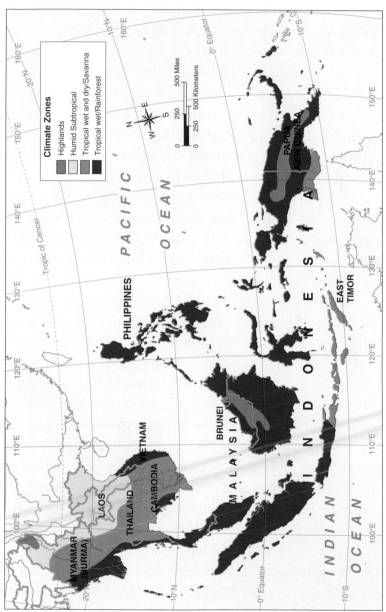

Almost all the countries of Southeast Asia are located in tropical climates. The equator passes through the islands of Indonesia, leaving about half of the country in the Southern Hemisphere. Throughout this region, temperatures are typically mild, and seasonal temperatures vary by only a few degrees.

months is about 2°F (1°C), ranging from 78° to 80°F (26° to 27°C). Most of the region never experiences frost. Oceans maintain a near-constant temperature; therefore, temperatures of lands that border the sea also are moderate. At high elevations, freezing conditions, year-round snow, and even glaciers (atop Indonesia's highest peaks) are commonplace. Here, as elsewhere, differences in elevation contribute to very sharp contrasts in conditions.

Precipitation is monotonous as well. Most of Indonesia and the Philippines, as well as the tip of the Malay Peninsula, receive more than 80 inches (200 centimeters) of rainfall per year. Several locations are among the world's wettest, drenched by up to 400 inches (1,000 centimeters) of precipitation per year. A mountain city on the island of Java experiences an average 322 days with thunderstorms each year. Some locations in the humid tropics experience slight seasonal variations in moisture, but drought conditions are rare.

Much of mainland Southeast Asia experiences a tropical climate marked by seasonal wet and dry conditions. During the four- to six-month dry season (during the "winter," or low-sun season), temperatures are generally warmer because of the lack of cloud cover. Occasionally, they rise above 100°F (38°C). Frost, although not common, can occur in the northernmost reaches of this climatic region. Northern Vietnam, Laos, and Burma have a climate much like that of the Southeastern United States: humid subtropical. Conditions are marked by warm, rainy summers and cool, wet winters. Much of this region also is mountainous, so temperatures are considerably lower than one would expect for these latitudes.

The Philippines lies in the pathway of powerful Pacific typhoons (hurricanes). These storms can be devastating: Winds can approach 200 miles (320 kilometers) per hour and drenching rains, often exceeding 40 inches (100 centimeters) during a storm's passing, can cause severe flooding. Along shorelines, wind-driven waves can reach 20 feet (6 meters) in height and destroy everything in their path as they surge ashore. In December 2004, two typhoons walloped the country, killing nearly 2,000 people and leaving hundreds of thousands homeless.

The ways of living in Southeast Asia are keenly attuned to the region's climatic conditions. Culturally, it is incorrect to refer to "tropical peoples," as if their way of life is somehow fashioned by the climate in which they live. It is true that, because of extreme isolation, some people in remote areas continue to have a very traditional lifestyle. Singapore and most other cities within the region, however, are just as developed and cosmopolitan as many cities in the West.

PLANT AND ANIMAL LIFE

No other ecosystem can match the abundance and diversity of plant and animal life found in the tropics. Southeast Asia is no exception. Almost the entire region was once covered by dense forests. Hundreds of tree species and thousands of other plants occupied an area as small as one square mile (2.5 square kilometers). In the humid tropics, some trees grew to 200 feet (60 meters). Below their dense canopy, a vast array of shade-tolerant tree species, as well as shrubs, bamboo, mosses, ferns, and countless other plant forms, could be found. Because plants need sunlight to thrive, the forest floor itself is often relatively open. Jungles—dense, almost impenetrable stands of vegetation—are found only in places where sunlight can reach the plants. Such conditions often exist around streams, roadways, agricultural fields, and other cleared areas. Savanna grasslands and scattered woodlands dominate the wet and dry tropics on the mainland. Some species become dormant during the dry season, and burning to clear land of dry vegetation is common. To the north, in the humid subtropics, mixed forests dominate.

The tropics and subtropics are home to an abundance of fauna. Rivers teem with fish, as does the sea. Fishing has been an important source of food (and employment) for thousands of years. On land, there are hundreds of bird species and types of insects. There also are some things that you might want to avoid!

The region is home to nearly 500 different species of snakes, many of which are deadly. Poisonous snakes include the king cobra, coral, banded krait, and several varieties of viper, and the ocean is home to sea snakes that are among the world's most toxic (fortunately, they are not aggressive). Tropical Southeast Asia also is home to the reticulated python, reportedly the world's largest snake. According to a Reuters news release in December 2003, a town in Java claimed to have a python that measured 48 feet, 7 inches (14.83 meters) long and 2.8 feet (.85 meter) in diameter and weighed 984 pounds (446 kilograms)!

The Indonesian islands of Komodo and Flores are home to the world's largest and most dangerous lizard—the Komodo dragon. A full grown Komodo can reach 10 feet (3 meters) in length and weigh more than 200 pounds (90 kilograms). The dragons can swim and run as fast as humans for short distances. When bitten, the prey dies slowly from infection-causing bacteria in the dragon's mouth.

ENVIRONMENTAL ISSUES

Southeast Asia, like many of the world's regions, is experiencing a variety of environmental problems. In some areas, particularly Vietnam and Cambodia, the environment has been ravaged by warfare. Many cities suffer from air and water pollution, garbage and raw sewage, and industrial waste. Traditionally, shifting cultivation was practiced throughout the region, and it continues today in many rural areas. Most tropical soils are very infertile because their nutrients have been removed by leaching (washing away by heavy rains). As a result, fields produce a good crop for only several years, after which farmers move their plots. Vegetation is cut, allowed to dry out, and then burned. The system has destroyed much of the original vegetation cover, and the burning often causes severe seasonal air pollution. Wildlife habitat,

Malaysian rain forest is being cleared. The expanding population, the search for fresh farmland, and the logging operations (both legal and illegal) contribute to the major deforestation throughout much of Southeast Asia.

too, has been destroyed or is threatened as populations swell and land clearing for farming expands.

Deforestation is a major problem throughout much of the region, particularly in Indonesia. Commercially valuable tree species such as teak, mahogany, and ebony attract both legal and illegal logging operations. Whether cleared for farming or commercial logging, the result is the same: Land is cleared, forests are destroyed, soil is exposed and easily eroded, and flooding becomes increasingly common as rainwater sweeps down bared hillsides. Natural forests also are being replaced with commercial crops, such as coconut, oil palm, and rubber plantations.

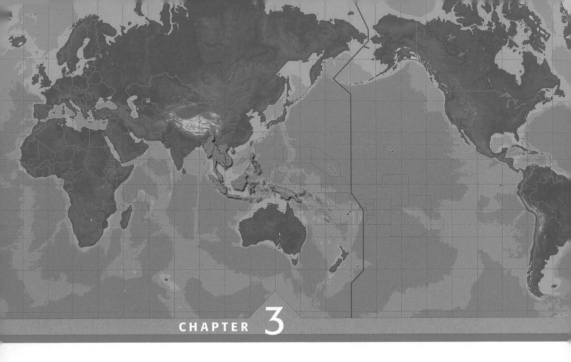

CHAPTER 3

Historical Geography

Water has played an important role in all societies because it is a necessity for life. In Southeast Asia, the role of water is perhaps more important historically than in other regions of the world. All of the region's countries, except for Laos, are bordered by the sea. For much of prehistory and early history, the oceans served as barriers that isolated people and cultures on the thousands of islands that are today Indonesia and the Philippines. On the Asian mainland, the Mekong River has been an artery of life for the peoples and cultures on the Peninsula for thousands of years.

Later in time, boats and navigational skills were developed. The oceans were no longer a wall that separated the people of Southeast Asia from outsiders. They instead became a water highway that soon

Water plays a major role in the culture of the mainland as well as the islands, as evidenced by these floating houses on the Mekong River in Vietnam.

connected the region to the world. Advanced technology allowed the waters to be used for trade, and, unfortunately, they were also used as a mechanism for foreign domination.

Because of the isolation, for much of history, there was little contact between region's people and other cultures. Ways of life within the region developed without much outside contact or influence until the arrival of outsiders from the Middle East, Europe, and elsewhere on mainland Asia.

EARLY PEOPLE

During the Ice Age, sea level dropped and much of today's island realm became an extension of mainland Southeast Asia. People migrated freely until, after the Ice Age, sea level rose and many found themselves living on islands. A human skull, named Java man, or *Pithecanthropus erectus,* by its finder, is reported to have lived in the area now known as Indonesia at least a half-million years ago and perhaps earlier.

Java man was found by Dutch doctor Eugene Dubois in 1891 on the island of Java. Dubois found a skullcap and teeth and tried to use the discovery to prove Charles Darwin's theory of evolution. Debate still rages over whether Java man provides meaningful evidence to support the theory of evolution because creationists and evolutionists disagree about the findings. Regardless, humanlike creatures have been in Southeast Asia for a very long time.

Evidence suggests that people have inhabited the Philippines for about 40,000 years. Ancestors of the Aeta people arrived on the islands at about the same time they arrived in Australia and Papua New Guinea. These first Filipinos were Australo-Melanesian people who were short with dark skin and curly hair. The Aeta people who developed from these early immigrants were hunting and gathering nomads who wandered widely in search of food.

The area that includes Laos, Cambodia, and Vietnam has been called Indochina for much of history. Throughout history, their pasts came in frequent contact with each other on the peninsula they share. Many early kingdoms, including Funan, Sikhottabong, and Chenla, sprang up along the Mekong River. This river is the world's twelfth longest, and it serves as a tremendous resource for many of today's Southeast Asian countries, including Thailand, Laos, Cambodia, Vietnam, Burma, and even China in East Asia. The river is so important that it is called Mae Nam Khong, or the "Mother of Waters," in Laos and Thailand and the Tonle Thom, or "Great Water," in Cambodia. This river's delta afforded rich soils where rice was cultivated before the first century A.D. The Mekong also provided fish, another staple of life for early people who lived in this region. In the early centuries of the first millennium, elaborate irrigation systems along the Mekong and its tributaries were set up for efficient production of rice. Today, more than 90 million people in Asia depend on the river.

THE RISE OF KINGDOMS

Geographer Carl Ortwin Sauer believed that agriculture—the deliberate planting and harvesting of crops and domestication of animals—may have begun in Southeast Asia. Certainly, farming was practiced here much earlier than in almost any other region in the world, and farming, one of the greatest cultural developments in all of human history, was responsible for many changes in the way people lived.

From early nomadic peoples who wandered in search of food and shelter, early civilizations arose as agriculture was introduced. This allowed people to stay in one area to supply their basic needs for food. Most of the agriculturally productive areas were in alluvial river valleys, such as that of the Mekong River, or on fertile coastal plains. With agriculture came early kingdoms that developed long before outsiders came via the sea to influence indigenous (native) cultures. Kingdoms with roots in India started to appear on the Malay Peninsula and in Indonesia in about A.D. 100. These kingdoms were spread more by trade than by the sword, and they extended the reach of many cultural and religious practices from India, including Buddhism and Hinduism. At first, these Indian kingdoms were small, with as many as 30 existing in the area that later became Malaysia. Smaller regional Indian kingdoms like Funan developed in Cambodia and Thailand along the Mekong River. Some kingdoms, such as Srivijaya, grew into mighty regional powers.

Srivijaya was located on the eastern part of what is today Sumatra. This kingdom became very powerful, and by the seventh century it had stretched to include most of Sumatra, western Java, and even large areas of the Malay Peninsula. People from China and other faraway places came to Srivijaya because it had become a key place for Mahayana Buddhists. The kingdom was the first to control the Strait of Malacca.

This position allowed it to become an important sea power. It was able to control trade in the region until the fourteenth century, when it was conquered by the Hindu kingdom of Majapahit, located in Java.

Culture in Vietnam was influenced more by China than by India. This cultural link remains even today, as China looms large just north of Vietnam. The Hung Dynasty was the first major empire in the region of Vietnam. It lasted until the third century B.C., when it was overthrown by the Thuc Kingdom and a new state called Au Lac was created. Au Lac was short lived: Under the leadership of military leader Trieu Da, China seized the region in 208 B.C., during the Qin Dynasty. In 206 B.C., the Han Dynasty was in power in China, and Trieu Da did not like its rule. He took the lands under his military command and created a kingdom called Nam Viet. By 111 B.C., however, the Han Dynasty had conquered the descendants of Trieu Da and incorporated the kingdom into the Han realm.

Islam is also an important historical influence in Southeast Asia. It arrived in Indonesia before 1292, when Marco Polo reported seeing it prevalent in the community of Perlak and assumed that it had been introduced earlier by Arab traders. In Malaysia, Islam was introduced from India during the early fourteenth century. The rise of Islam also gave rise to the powerful Islamic kingdom of Melaka, which was situated on the Malay Peninsula.

Legend holds that Melaka was founded in 1400 by a prince from the kingdom of Srivijaya who fled to the Malay Peninsula after being persecuted by the Majapahit kingdom on Indonesia. The prince had been a Hindu-Buddhist but converted to Islam and changed his name to Iskandar Syah. Melaka became a sultanate and major Islamic power during the second half of the fifteenth century. Melaka then went on the military offensive and added lands in Sumatra and took others from Thailand. States on the Malay Peninsula such as Kedah, Pahang, Johor, and Muar also fell to Melaka because the sultanate controlled both sides of the Strait of Malacca, including the island of Singapore. Trading was a major endeavor of the empire as Melaka grew into a bustling city with a population of more than 40,000. Something was about to happen, however, something that would change the fate of Melaka and its empire, as well as all of Southeast Asia.

ARRIVAL OF THE FIRST EUROPEANS

On September 1, 1509, Melaka had a new visitor. A Portuguese fleet under the command of Admiral Diego Lopez de Sequeira entered the city's harbor. This was the first European power to land in Malay waters, and the contact marked the beginning of an abrupt change in the history of Southeast Asia. The first visitors to Southeast Asia from India had come in like a whisper, quietly introducing Hinduism and Buddhism; later visitors, however, often came in like a windstorm, with the interests of conquering and controlling new lands and converting them into colonies.

The Malays were at first intrigued by the Portuguese but soon became resentful of the new visitors and conducted a surprise attack on Sequeira's small fleet. The Portuguese escaped but lost two of their ships and about 20 sailors. One sailor to escape with Sequeira was Ferdinand Magellan, a man later credited with being the first to circumnavigate the world. The Portuguese returned in 1511 with a much larger and more powerful fleet. This fleet was led by Alphonso d'Albuquerque, who quickly led his forces to victory by seizing Melaka. On this voyage, Albuquerque also stopped in the Spice Islands. The Portuguese were motivated only in part by revenge for Sequeira's besieged earlier exit; they also recognized the strategic location of Melaka in relation to the Spice Islands, which are now part of Indonesia. The Catholic Portuguese ousted the Muslim leaders in Melaka. Islam had been a problem for

Porta de Santiago is the gate of the Portuguese fortress A'Famosa, built in 1511 on the orders of Alfonso de Albuquerque, the Portuguese Viceroy of India who had led the capture of the city of Malacca. The gate is the only part of the fortress remaining today.

Portugal and Spain since the Iberian Peninsula was invaded by Moors in A.D. 711.

EUROPEAN INFLUENCE EXPANDS

European powers quickly entered Southeast Asia in search of natural resources, spices, markets, and other sources of wealth. Spices, particularly black pepper, cloves, and nutmeg, were especially valuable in Europe, where traders could expect to earn a huge profit, as much as 10,000 percent, according to some sources. The Spice Islands became a very precious source of wealth to foreign interests. Magellan arrived in the Philippines in 1521 and was killed by natives during his stay. The Spanish arrived in the Spice Islands in 1560 and turned the Philippines into a colony five years later. The British presence entered the region with Sir Francis Drake, who visited various islands in Indonesia during his trip in 1579–1580. The Dutch arrived in the Spice Islands with four ships in 1596. The race was on for the riches to be found in Southeast Asia.

These European powers were competing not only in Southeast Asia but were also busily laying claim to lands and resources throughout much of the world. Dutch and British interest in the Spice Islands was an extension of this larger sphere of competition. Spurred on by the tremendous value of spices in European markets, the Dutch moved quickly to establish a permanent presence in the region. They did so by chartering the Dutch East India Company, or Vereenigde Oost-Indische Compagnie (VOC), in 1602. The company's task was to control all spice trade in the archipelago. Dutch warships quickly pushed the Portuguese out of most of the Spice Islands. The Dutch then moved to consolidate their power and turned the lands under their control into a colony. Undaunted, the British also set up trading posts in some areas of the Spice Islands in 1611.

The local populations did not simply accept the outsiders; they often fought back in an attempt to repel the European intruders. Locals attempted to throw the VOC out of Jakarta in 1529, but the Dutch responded by burning the city to the ground. The Europeans had vastly superior ships and weapons that made almost all local resistance efforts unsuccessful. Skirmishes usually resulted in thousands of people being killed, enslaved, or injured. Resistance was futile in the face of superior technology.

Dutch rule in Indonesia was often harsh. Local people were forced to work in almost slavelike conditions, and thousands starved to death in the rice-producing area of Cirebon in

1849–1850. The Dutch determined which crops would be raised and how much would be produced. This control was imposed as they shrewdly tried to keep the prices of certain spices and other crops artificially high so that profit margins would be greater. The Dutch also brought a degree of arrogance with them: They believed that they were superior to the local people. None of this endeared the Dutch to the Indonesians.

Indonesia received a short reprieve from Dutch rule in 1811. The Netherlands became involved in protecting their homeland from an invasion of Napoleon Bonaparte's forces. The British and Dutch negotiated an agreement whereby the British would rule the Dutch colony during the European occupation of Holland by French forces. As agreed, the British returned the Spice Islands to the Dutch in 1816. The rule of the islands by Sir Thomas Stamford Raffles and the British provided a time of enlightened colonial rule that lasted only five years before the Dutch returned. Raffles initiated reforms in slavery, introduced limited self-government, and provided for efforts in land reform and crop selection by locals.

Having completed his work successfully in the Spice Islands, Raffles was soon to be appointed to another position of importance. This assignment was in Singapore, where Raffles set up a British trading post in the key port city. The Dutch viewed this situation with dismay, because they also had interest in controlling the Malacca Strait.

BRITISH INFLUENCE EXPANDS

Raffles had previously been stationed in Penang (Malaysia) and spoke the Malay language fluently. With his extended service in the Spice Islands and on the Malay Peninsula, he understood the importance of Singapore and, in 1818, convinced his superiors in India that a trading post sponsored by the British East India Company would be strategically important. In a letter he later sent to a friend, he said that Singapore "is by far the most important station in the East; and, as far as naval superiority and commercial interests are concerned, of much higher value than whole continents of territory."

British presence on the mainland began in Malaya with the establishment of a port in Penang in 1786 and their gaining of control over Melaka in 1795. Gradually, on the Malay Peninsula, the British created the Federated Malay States in a piecemeal fashion that was completed in 1909. After World War II, the two final pieces of the Malaysia puzzle fell into place when the British took Sarawak and Sabah on the island of Borneo.

Brunei was first visited by the Spanish and the Portuguese. The British, however, left the most lasting mark on the country. With the increased British influence on neighboring Sarawak, the sultanate of Brunei became a protectorate in 1888. In 1929, with the discovery of petroleum, Brunei became even more important to the British and others. In 1963, Brunei expressed some interest in becoming a part of the Federation of Malaysia, but this was rejected. The country finally gained independence from the British in 1984.

The British also ruled Burma after gaining control of the region in a series of three wars with France in the nineteenth century. By 1886, after the French were defeated, the British put all of Burma under the British *raj* (ruler) of India. Burma remained under British control until 1937, when it became a self-governing British protectorate. Full independence finally came in 1948.

FRENCH INVOLVEMENT

In addition to their early presence in Burma, the French were longtime colonial players in Indochina. They had an economic interest in Southeast Asia, but they also wanted to spread their language, religion, and other traits of French culture. For a long time, part of the region was called French Indochina; it included Laos, Cambodia, and Vietnam. French leadership in China started to push for a greater French role in Southeast Asia in 1841. In response, France stepped up its naval presence in the region and started military actions in support of French religious and economic interests. In 1847, they attacked the city of Da Nang, Vietnam. Ten thousand Vietnamese were killed, and five Vietnamese ships were destroyed in the fighting. In the decades that followed, France worked to remain a world power with a colonial empire by extending its reach farther into Vietnam, Cambodia, and, finally, Laos.

Through a series of battles and treaties with lopsided advantages for the French, Vietnam finally completely fell when the Citadel, in the city of Hue, was taken in 1883. Wasting little time, the French established the Union of Indochina, which also included Cambodia, in 1887.

Cambodia had long been trapped between the regional powers in Thailand and Vietnam. Seeking protection from these neighbors, Cambodia under King Norodom agreed to a treaty that guaranteed the monarch French protection against his neighbors. In return, the French received the right to explore and exploit the kingdom's vast mineral and forest resources. This relationship evolved and, by 1887, Cambodia was also rolled into the Union of Indochina.

Laos was added to French Indochina in 1893. Siam (now Thailand) had long been a regional power in Laos but knew that it could not compete militarily against the French. Thus, the French made moves to seize key locations in Laos in the years preceding its entry into the Union of Indochina. They brought military pressure on Siam, which resulted in the country relinquishing its claims on Laos in 1893. The final piece was in place, and now French Indochina included Vietnam, Cambodia, and Laos. The French colonial era in Southeast Asia lasted until 1953.

SPAIN CLAIMS THE PHILIPPINES

Spain was the world's preeminent naval power for much of the sixteenth century, and its colonial reach extended around the world. The country's naval strength allowed it to proceed in its quest for colonies—until the defeat of its Armada by the British in 1588. Spain's first entry in Southeast Asia was provided by Magellan, who landed on the island of Cebu in the Philippines in 1521. Only a month after his landing, he was killed by the local people. In contrast to Magellan's death and unlike many other European countries, Spain's entry into the Philippines was relatively peaceful: The locals offered little resistance. The Spanish presence in Southeast Asia was primarily felt in the Philippines, which became a colony in 1565. Even the name, the Philippines, is of Spanish origin: The country was named after King Philip II, who ruled Spain from 1556 to 1598.

The Spanish had three major goals for its colony in the Philippines: First, they wanted to have a role in the region's spice trade; second, they hoped to convert the local people to Christianity; and third, they wanted to develop contact with Japan and China that would support the development of Christianity in those countries. The second goal was the only one they achieved: Today, the Philippines is 83 percent Catholic.

As Spain's power declined, other colonial powers started infringing on the Philippines. The British briefly captured Manila in 1762, but the city and surrounding area were returned to Spanish rule in 1764 by the Treaty of Paris. By the late nineteenth century, there were local uprisings against the colonial rule of the Spanish. Most assaults were ineffective, and, generally, the dissidents were forced to conduct guerrilla warfare activities that met with little success.

Spanish rule in the Philippines ended after three centuries, when the United States Navy easily defeated Spain's fleet in Manila Harbor on May 1, 1898. Local rebels had sided with the United States and assisted in the quick defeat of the Spanish forces around Manila. After the U.S. and rebel victory, Germany, France, Japan, and the British sent warships into Manila's harbor. Germany alone had eight warships in the harbor and acted very aggressively in its blatant attempts to provoke a conflict with the United States in order to secure a colonial foothold in Southeast Asia. The United States Navy in Manila Bay was under Commodore George Dewey. He confronted the Germans' aggressive actions, and Germany backed down. In the Treaty of Paris of 1898, Spain ceded the Philippines to the United States. In return, the United States paid Spain 20 million dollars. With this treaty, the United States emerged as the newest member of the colonial club in Southeast Asia.

AMERICAN INVOLVEMENT IN THE REGION

Philippine rebels who had been allies of the Americans in the Spanish-American War soon realized that the war's results would not bring independence. This was apparent because the Americans kept the rebels out of Manila just after the victory in 1898. Filipinos were also angry about being bought and sold by colonial powers in the Treaty of Paris. Thus, Filipino resistance to the United States as the new colonial master started immediately.

The United States was a different type of colonial master, however. From the beginning of U.S. rule, the primary goal was to prepare the Philippines for the transition from colonial status to independence. The United States believed that the Philippines was not ready for independence in 1898 because of its lack of experience in self-governance. In 1907, a two-house legislature was implemented, and, in 1934, the U.S. Congress passed the Tydings-McDuffie Act, which established a ten-year timeline for independence.

THAILAND AVOIDS COLONIAL CONTROL

Thailand was the sole country that avoided colonization during this era. This was accomplished through the kingdom of Ayutthaya's trade treaties with the Portuguese who visited in 1511 and the Dutch who came in 1592. Trade arrangements also were developed with British and French trading companies. Diplomats were sent to Paris and The Hague, in Holland. The Thais proved to be masters at playing the colonial powers against each other. This strategy successfully kept the country from being colonized.

The sea provided the access European powers used to consolidate their power in Southeast Asia. The sea power and both naval and military technology of Portugal, Holland, Spain, England, France, Germany, and the United States made conquests possible, and all of Southeast Asia except Thailand felt the immense impact of foreign colonization and dominance. By the end of the 1930s, Europe was facing war with Germany and the Axis powers. How would this affect Southeast Asia?

From Colonies
to Countries

World War II punctuates the history of Southeast Asia like an exclamation point! The war provided the context for stunning changes during, and perhaps more importantly, after the conflict. Japan is an island neighbor to Southeast Asia. Until the second half of the nineteenth century, the country had deliberately kept itself isolated from the rest of the world. This isolation was originally intended to keep the country secure from outside threats. It also kept the country isolated from advances in military and other technology. This changed quickly in 1853, with the arrival of the U.S. Navy led by Commodore Matthew C. Perry. Perry entered Tokyo Harbor with the intent of opening Japan to trade. Perry's arsenal pried open Japan's closed door.

Japan was thrown into political turmoil by the Perry-inspired events. It rapidly moved forward from an era of traditional *shogun* and *samurai* dominance to the Meiji era of modernization. The Japanese saw European powers scrambling to build colonial empires as sources of trade and natural resources. The country responded quickly by building its own naval fleet and began to acquire additional lands. It expanded into parts of China in 1894 and Russia in 1904–1905. Its defeat of Russia was the first time an Asian country defeated a modern European power.

Emboldened by its successes and a continuing thirst for an empire, Japan continued to expand and grew stronger in the Pacific region as Europe and the United States became immersed in World War II. The thirst of the Japanese military for natural resources and colonies was unquenchable. Southeast Asia was now in range, and Japan knew that the sea held the key to power in the Asia-Pacific region. Only the United States remained as a major barrier to Japan's dream of expansion.

Because the sea was the key to Japan's dream of an empire, the Japanese military believed that a strike at the heart of America's naval presence was necessary. On December 7, 1941, Japan struck out violently with an unprovoked attack on Pearl Harbor in Hawaii. A few hours later, the Japanese mounted a similar strike on the U.S. air and naval presence in Manila in the Philippines. U.S. or British military installations in Malaya, Hong Kong, Thailand, Wake Island, and Guam were all attacked by Japan before December 10, 1941, as Japan's coordinated plan was implemented. In the Philippines and Hawaii, Japan's surprise attack caught U.S. Air Force planes on the ground, positioned as easy targets. Ships were sunk in the harbors as Japan carried out its attempt to strike a fatal blow and neutralize the United States's air and sea presence in the Pacific region.

Another reason for the strike was Japan's immediate need for resources. Japan had started moving into Indochina by mid-1941, and its presence had caught the attention of European colonial powers. Finally moved to action, the British and Dutch imposed an embargo on the shipping of strategic materials to Japan. Many believed that this embargo, imposed in mid-1941, threatened Japan because the country was facing shortages in oil and other key natural resources. Facing this dilemma, Japan made plans to neutralize the United States's air and naval forces in the Pacific. Thus, the attacks on Pearl Harbor and other locations paved the way for Japan's move into resource-rich Southeast Asia.

With the preemptive Japanese strikes in the Pacific, there was little left to contain Japan's surge into Southeast Asia. Like autumn leaves falling in a windstorm, the colonies in Southeast quickly fell to the powerful Japanese forces. Thailand was attacked but chose to become a Japanese ally against the Western allied forces rather than be occupied by Japan. Others resisted to varying degrees, but all of Southeast Asia was under Japan's rule by 1942.

The Japanese occupation proved to be a somewhat mixed blessing to the people of Southeast Asia. On the negative side, the occupation by Japanese forces was often very harsh. In some places, the Japanese rule was harsher than that of the colonial occupations: Tens of thousands of people died of starvation or by working as slave laborers in camps under the Japanese task masters. Others died trying to resist the advance of the Japanese military juggernaut. Women in the Philippines, Indonesia, Burma, and other places were forced to become "comfort" women, or prostitutes. Data show that more than 200,000 women were forced into prostitution during the Japanese occupation of Southeast Asia.

Japanese occupation also had some positive effects. Southeast Asia (except Thailand) had been under the grip of foreign colonial powers for decades or even centuries. Japan's slogan in 1942 was, "The leader of Asia, the protector of Asia, the light of Asia." This statement summarized a political strategy of Japan's, which was to play toward the spirit of nationalism that had been rising in Southeast Asian colonies before World War II. This message played to many individuals and political figures in places such as Indonesia, Vietnam, and the Philippines, where nationalists were trying to cast off the European and American colonial powers. World War II had shown that these powers were not invincible. This factor and Japan's promise to support independence movements helped promote nationalist movements in the region.

With the Battle of Midway, the tide of World War II in the Pacific started to turn toward the United States and the Allies. Island-hopping their way across the Pacific toward Japan, the Allies methodically pushed the Japanese forces back to their homeland. Fearing thousands of casualties in an attempt to invade Japan, President Truman chose to use atomic bombs on the cities of Hiroshima and Nagasaki. The bombs' ferocity was unleashed on August 6 and 9, respectively, in 1945. Emperor Hirohito surrendered for Japan a few days later, on August 14, 1945, when a tape of his voice, heard by the Japanese people for the first time, was played on the radio. Many in the Japanese military wanted to keep fighting even though the situation was hopeless. To this end, right-wing army and navy leaders attempted to take the emperor hostage on the night of his surrender to the Allies. The attempt failed and the war was finally over.

NATIONALISM AND NEW NATIONS

As the curtains closed on World War II, European countries sought to regain control over their former colonies. Circumstances had changed, however. The myth of invincibility of the European colonial masters had been shattered by World War II, when the French and Dutch had been easily overrun by Germany and the Axis powers. Germany and Italy had lost the war and were not a colonial threat anymore. The British had suffered greatly during the war, and Spain had lost influence because of favoring the Axis during the early years of the war. In addition, many in Southeast Asia had fought alongside the Allies to help defeat Japan in Southeast Asia. They believed that they now deserved independence.

Indonesia

The Netherlands tried to reassert power in the Dutch East Indies immediately after the war, but the country faced stiff resistance from an emboldened nationalist movement that declared independence on August 17, 1945. Sukarno assumed the presidency. The Dutch were greatly weakened by the effects of World War II, but they tried to confront the Indonesian nationalists militarily. Fighting broke out as the Dutch tried to remove the nationalists from the islands of Java and Sumatra.

The United States finally stepped in and pressured the Dutch to allow Indonesia's independence. This was done under the darkening cloud of Soviet Communism, which was spreading from the USSR to China and threatening to gain a foothold in Indonesia. The United States was concerned about this "Red menace" and feared a domino effect in which one country after another would fall under Communist domination. Americans saw Sukarno and the nationalist movement as anti-Communist because they had fought against Communists in Indonesia. On December 27, 1949, the Netherlands finally transferred all powers to the Republic of Indonesia and Jakarta was established as the capital.

Indochina

In Vietnam, Ho Chi Minh and others helped defeat the Japanese. Shortly after the end of the war, he declared Vietnam's independence for the new Democratic Republic of Vietnam. France, supported by the United States, Great Britain, India, and others, was encouraged to retain control over Indochina and Vietnam, specifically because of its strategic position and its importance as a producer of agricultural products. Both French and Chinese interests were involved in Vietnam. After the war, however, Vietnamese nationalists were anxious to be rid of these foreign influences. What followed was a war between the nationalists and France called the First Indochina War. The conflict began in 1946 and lasted until 1954. After the conflict subsided, Vietnam was divided into two parts by the Geneva Agreements of 1954, which established the 17th parallel as the boundary between North Vietnam and South Vietnam. A demilitarized zone (DMZ) was created between the north and south. The French also agreed to move their forces south of the 17th parallel.

A number of parties had helped shape the Geneva Agreements. Participants in the decision included the Democratic Republic of Vietnam (DRV), the Associated State of Vietnam (ASV), France, Cambodia, Laos, Great Britain, China, the Soviet Union, and the United States. None of the parties was especially pleased with the outcome of the agreements: There were officially two Vietnams, the DRV in the north and the ASV in the south. These were referred to as North Vietnam and South Vietnam during the Second Indochina War.

Communists had already taken over the government in China and had established the People's Republic of China (PRC). They had been aiding Hanoi, in the north, in its war against the French. Thus, Ho Chi Minh had become more closely tied to the Communists and the support they received from both the PRC and the Soviet Union. South Vietnam was tied more closely to the West and to the United States. France exited North Vietnam by the Geneva Agreements of 1954, and the United States saw an important threat: Communist North Vietnam started to make major intrusions into the South Vietnam. They also started to foster insurrections against the ARV government.

In 1961, U.S. President John F. Kennedy started to increase aid to South Vietnam in the hope of fending off the Communist intrusions. By 1964, however, the DRV controlled almost half of South Vietnam. The same year, the United States claimed

Paratroopers of the French-Indochinese Union army are watched by their comrades as Operation Castor gets underway, on November 20, 1953, in the hilltop district northwest of Hanoi. Several paratrooper units were launched in a campaign to strengthen the garrison of Dien Bien Phu.

that the DRV had shelled its ships in the Gulf of Tonkin. This spurred President Lyndon Johnson to request a resolution from Congress that gave him authority to prevent further aggression in South Vietnam. In response, the Soviet Union pledged additional support for North Vietnam. The Second Indochina War was now on.

By 1967, half a million U.S. troops were in Vietnam and heavy air bombing was taking place in Hanoi and other strategic locations in North Vietnam. In backing South Vietnam, the United States had developed a record of backing leaders unpopular with the Vietnamese people. By 1968, with the Tet Offensive, the tide began to turn against the United States and

South Vietnam. In 1969, the United States attacked Cambodia to remove Vietnamese bases that were operating just across the common border. Other DRV supply trails had run through Laos. The expanded war did not end the successes of North Vietnam because the United States began to grow tired of the war. At home, there was rising and vocal political dissent to U.S. involvement. Ultimately, the United States withdrew its forces and North Vietnam succeeded in defeating South Vietnam. The country was formally reunited in 1976.

Laos and Cambodia also had been parts of French In-dochina and were affected greatly by the wars in Vietnam. In Laos, the North Vietnamese had supported the Pathet Lao, first in their resistance to the French and later against the Royal Lao Army. Laos received independence from the French in 1954, but the situation remained complicated under the new royal government. When Vietnam invaded Laos in 1959, it was as-sisting the Communist Pathet Lao. The Pathet Lao threw out the monarchy and assumed control of the country in 1975, the same year that North Vietnam defeated South Vietnam. Laos was now under Communist rule and called the Lao People's Democratic Republic. To many observers, it appeared that the "domino theory" about the spread of Communism in South-east Asia was very much a threat.

After World War II, Cambodia followed a different course than the other parts of Indochina did. After the war, Prince Norodom Sihanouk worked carefully with the French to arrange a successful transition to full independence, which was granted in 1953. In 1970, the Sihanouk government was over-thrown in a military coup led by General Lon Nol.

Nol's government was called the Khmer Republic, and it, too, was caught up in the whirlwind of the Vietnam War. Communists that were called the Khmer Rouge, led by Pol Pot, eventually seized control of the government in 1975. This started the deadly Democratic Kampuchea period, during which more than 3 million people are thought to have been

HU-1D (Huey) helicopters lift from a landing zone after U.S. paratroopers of the 173rd Airborne Brigade, moving toward the road, were lifted into the area northeast of Ben Cat, 30 miles north of Saigon, South Vietnam, on September 14, 1965, during the Vietnam War.

killed by the Khmer Rouge government. This horror inspired the 1984 movie *The Killing Fields.* The Pol Pot regime used repression in every form to terrorize citizens and create rule by fear. Pol Pot's government banned virtually all public institutions: Stores, banks, hospitals, schools, and religion were forbidden. Even the family came under attack; children often were forcibly separated from their parents. Everyone was forced to work 12 to 14 hours per day, 7 days per week under often horrifying conditions. By the late 1970s, Kampuchea started to persecute Vietnamese people in Cambodia and it conducted military intrusions into Thailand and Vietnam.

Vietnam's 1979 retaliatory invasion was not a surprise, and it served as a relief to most Cambodians because it marked the end of Pol Pot's reign of terror.

Singapore and Malaysia

Singapore and Malaysia share a history of British colonization and are close in geographic proximity—Singapore is connected to the mainland by a short causeway. Singapore had long served as an entry point for workers going to the Malay Peninsula to work in extracting resources that were usually exported through Singapore. Economic development came quickly to Singapore, which was rapidly becoming a hub for banking and business interests in the region. Malaysia was considered an economic treasure chest, with rich stores of rubber, tin, and many other valuable resources.

Singapore housed an important British naval base that was built in 1923 with the partial intent of providing a regional counterforce to Japan. This made the colony a strategic target for the Japanese during World War II, when they surprised the British by attacking overland through the Malay Peninsula. The occupation of Singapore was harsh: Tens of thousands of people were tortured or killed. The memory of this occupation is very evident even today in Singapore, where the Civilian War Memorial towers high in the city. This shrine, sometimes called the "chopsticks" memorial because of its unusual shape, is dedicated to civilians who died during the Japanese occupation.

During the 1950s, the British took steps to increase Singapore's autonomy and self-rule. Full independence was not granted until 1965, after a failed two-year experiment that included having Singapore in the Federation of Malaysia. With the Federation being unsalvageable, Lee Kuan Yew helped lead Singapore to independence. He also served as the country's first prime minister. Under Lee's guidance, Singapore became a global financial and industrial powerhouse, despite having almost no natural resources. Lee accomplished this by ruling with

The Civilian War Memorial in Singapore is nicknamed the "chopsticks" memorial because of its shape. It was built in memory of the tens of thousands tortured and killed during the Japanese occupation of Singapore in World War II.

great authority, which allowed him to set in motion many of the laws that some people criticize as too restrictive. He stepped down as prime minister in 1990, but the country has continued to prosper.

Malaysian nationalism increased greatly after World War II because the British were no longer viewed as invincible. Tunku Abdul Rahman helped lead the colony forward in its resistance to the British, and independence was realized in 1957. He was the first prime minister in the Federation of Malaya (1957–1963) and of Malaysia (1963–1970). In the early 1960s, he tried to create a federation with Singapore that failed in 1965. This effort had threatened Indonesia's regional quest for lands under Sukarno and resulted in raids on Sarawak and Sabah, both of which wanted to join Malaysia. This, along with other factors, helped convince the Federation partners that the union with Singapore was untenable.

Malaysia moved forward significantly in the economic realm under Prime Minister Mahathir bin Mohammed, who served from 1981 to 2003. His vision and actions helped transform Malaysia from a natural resource provider to a provider of world-class technology.

The Philippines

The impetus for Philippine independence was the Tydings-McDuffie Act, which was passed by the United States Congress in 1934. Under the terms of this act, the Philippines was to receive its independence a decade later. Japanese occupation of the islands during World War II delayed this transition until 1946, when the country became self-governing. After Philippine independence was achieved, the United States assisted with the fledgling country's reconstruction from the devastation created by the Japanese invasion and occupation.

The Philippines and the United States maintained strong economic and military relationships for several decades after World War II. The United States had a strong strategic interest in the Pacific region because of the rising Communist tide in Indochina and other areas of Southeast Asia. The Philippines presented a desirable location for air and naval bases, and, in return, these bases provided the Philippines with badly needed hard currency. However, a number of incidents in the late 1960s, related to Marcos' support of U.S. involvement in Vietnam and the stationing of U.S. troops in the Philippines, started turning Filipino attitudes against the U.S. presence. By 1991, all American bases in the Philippines had been closed.

Democratic rule prevailed in the Philippines until the arrival of Ferdinand Marcos, who was elected president in 1965. In 1969, he became the first Filipino president reelected to the office. Marcos, however, was limited by the Constitution—a virtual clone of the American document—to two four-year terms. To retain power, Marcos established a parliamentary system. This change allowed him to become prime minister and serve indefinitely. Opposition quickly arose against Marcos, who responded by declaring martial law over the entire country. He turned the country into a dictatorship that was subject to his orders and unrestrained power. Political opponents, including Benigno Aquino, and journalists were arrested and jailed as martial rule continued from 1972 to 1981.

Benigno Aquino likely would have been elected president in 1972 if elections had taken place. Instead, he was locked up for seven years, until he was allowed to go to the United States for medical treatment in 1980. While in the United States, Aquino was involved with the Philippine government in exile. Against the advice of many, including Imelda Marcos, wife of the dictator, Aquino returned to the Philippines in 1983. He was quickly killed by an alleged Communist gunman. Allegations of a conspiracy by the military with possible involvement by Ferdinand Marcos and his wife followed the assassination. Soon, millions were demonstrating in the streets and Filipino People Power was born. The demonstrations proved that Benigno Aquino was an even stronger opponent to Marcos in death than in life.

People Power forced Marcos to resign from office in 1986, and Aquino's wife, Corazon, took office as the seventh president of the Philippines. Democratic elections have been conducted in the country since her election.

Burma and Thailand

Burma was a major stage for fighting during World War II. The Allies, led in Burma by the British, worked to draw a "line" in Asia in the country of Burma. This line was drawn so that Japan would not be able to invade India and create an Asian empire. This crossroads location meant that many major battles took place in Burma, then a British protectorate. Indians who served under British officers provided much of the military effort. In addition, the famous Burma Road was built by the Allies to connect India and China, where at the time, the Chinese Nationalist Army was also fighting Japanese forces. This vital route provided the Nationalists with the supplies necessary to continue fighting. This meant that large numbers of Japanese military personnel had to be shifted to the Chinese front and could not be used elsewhere. The rugged terrain and climate in Burma took a huge toll on both sides during the war. The armies struggled against not only each other for survival but also against the unforgiving environment; torrential monsoon rains, malaria, and typhoid fever were only a few of the hazards.

The Burmese people supported the British during the war. They had been promised independence prior to the war with the establishment of the protectorate. Thus, Burma became independent soon after the war in 1948. A parliamentary government ruled until 1962, when the military under the leadership of General Ne Win staged a coup. The general threw out the democratically elected leaders and established a one-party socialist state. Finally, in 1988, massive public demonstrations forced Ne Win to resign from office.

Life under Ne Win's regime had been horrible. Torture and other human rights abuses were commonplace, and re-

A U.S. supply convoy, operating regularly between the Burmese railhead of Lashio and the Chinese city of Guiyang, is making its way along the famous 21 curves of the Burma Road, in the Yunnan province in southwestern China, March 26, 1945.

sistance was crushed by the military, which always stepped in to control the demonstrations. The methods were brutal. On one occasion, an estimated 10,000 demonstrators were killed in Rangoon (Yangon) when the military fired on them with machine guns. Despite this brutal power, the protestors forced the military to conduct general elections. In the elections, Aung San Suu Kyi won an overwhelming victory. Instead of taking office, she and other party leaders were promptly placed under house arrest by the military regime.

Burma's repressive regime has remained in power since 1990, although Aung San Suu Kyi and others are working to create a democratic country. Aung San Suu Kyi won the Nobel Peace Price in 1991 and has remained at the heart of the Burmese resistance. The military government continues to make promises of democratic elections and constitutional reform, but action has not followed. New talks were started by the military in 2000, but little progress has been made in democratizing the country.

Thailand traveled a course unlike any other country in Southeast Asia during World War II. As a coerced partner of Japan, it did not suffer as much as its neighbors did. Joined with Japan, Thailand also hoped that it might regain its former lands in Cambodia and Laos if the Allies were defeated. Thailand's alliance with Japan was resisted at first militarily, but finally the country gave Japan access to its lands for the ground invasion of Burma and Malaya. Thailand's course differed in still another way. Unlike other countries in Southeast Asia, it had not been colonized before the war by European powers. This allowed Thailand to have greater freedom in determining its political, economic, and social directions before, during, and after World War II.

Thailand's declaration of war on the United States came in 1942. The Thai ambassador in Washington, D.C., refused to deliver the declaration to the U.S. government, however; therefore, the United States never retaliated by declaring war on

Thailand. This strange turn of events meant that the Allies never invaded Thailand. Instead, Japan began to treat Thailand badly as the war effort waned. This turned public opinion against the military-tainted Thai government of Luang Plaek Phibunsongkhram (Phibun for short), who had served as prime minister since 1938. In 1944, Phibun was thrown out of office and replaced by a civilian government led by an intellectual named Pridi Phanomyong.

Thailand today is a constitutional monarchy with a blending of democratic and royal elements. The absolute monarchy ended in 1932, when a military coup forced the creation of a constitution. For many years after the coup, the military had a strong influence on government, which it even controlled on occasion. During World War II, the monarchy secretly opposed Japan. When King Phumiphon came to the throne in 1950, he promoted a pro-Western government. This pro-West attitude allowed the United States to house troops in Thailand during the Vietnam War.

A new constitution created in 1997 made Thailand much more democratic. The military continues to watch over the government, but its role is considerably diminished from what it had during much of the twentieth century. Thailand had the world's highest economic growth rate from 1985 to 1995 but then suffered a brief, steep economic downturn during 1997 and 1998. Steady growth has taken place since that time as political stability has enhanced Thailand's economic opportunities.

The role of water and the sea continues to be of importance to Southeast Asia. Much of history has been influenced by how people have used the seas. The past shows that people have used the seas for both cooperation and conflict, as well as for trade and terror. With the rise of ASEAN and various other international agreements, perhaps the future will allow for continued cooperation without seaborne conflicts.

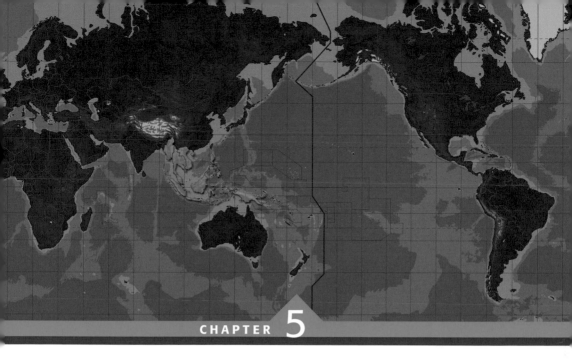

CHAPTER 5

People and Cultures

Southeast Asia has an amazing diversity of humankind. Most of the major religions of the world have strong roots in some part of the region. Hundreds of languages flourish. Some aboriginal tongues are thousands of years old and are spoken by small numbers of people. Others are spoken by millions. Non-native languages also thread across the region because French, English, Spanish, and even Dutch colonists brought their languages to the region. Deep in the cultural soul of each of these nations beats the heart of a rich culture with music, clothing, dance, foods, and other traditions that have a history in the early people of the region.

This region is one of considerable cultural diversity, home to some remote and traditional peoples whose lives provide a sharp

This is a busy market in Bali, Indonesia. Despite the encroachment of many foreign businesses (McDonald's, Orange Julius, etc.), the local marketplace remains a vibrant source of local economy.

contrast to many well-educated people whose lives are "modern" in every respect. In terms of outlook, some people live in areas that remained isolated from outsiders for centuries. Some people who live in parts of Indonesia and Malaysia have had the world on their doorstep for centuries, countries in search of the rich spice trade and the adventures of world exploration. Today, some of the region continues to borrow heavily from other cultures. In Singapore, for example, a visitor quickly finds McDonald's, Orange Julius, Kentucky Fried Chicken, Pizza Hut, Taco Bell, 7-Eleven, and many other familiar businesses. Yet the heart of Singapore has cultural elements drawn from China, India, Malaysia, Japan, and even Great Britain. This former

British colony has a mixed population that reflects the colonial heritage and the movement of people that has taken place in Southeast Asia. The city is very cosmopolitan, ranking with the finest European and American cities in terms of the availability of trendy clothing, electronics, cars, and other consumable items. The surface shows this trendy urban exterior, but the core of Singapore, as elsewhere in Southeast Asia, rests on old traditions, religions, and cultural patterns.

Singapore is not typical of the entire region. In some places, such as Burma and areas within Cambodia, Laos, and Vietnam, life occasionally seems to have taken a trip many decades back in time because little has changed in recent years. In Burma, time seems to have stood still. Because of its oppressive military government, many countries, including the United States, do not maintain relations with that nation. Other countries fall somewhere between Singapore and Burma. Traditional ways of living remain in each, particularly in cities, but the degree of modernity varies with the influence of urban living and the degree of contact with outside cultures.

This chapter investigates the people and cultures of Southeast Asia. It includes a look at key cultural elements in the region, including demographics, language, religion, food, and the arts, as well as examining some of the new cultural trends that affect the region.

PEOPLE OF SOUTHEAST ASIA

The ethnic mix in Southeast Asia is great. There are Chinese, Malay, Khmer, Burmese, and Vietnamese, as well as Thai, Hmong, Indian, Madurese, Javanese, Sundanese, Lao Loum, Lao Theung, and many other peoples. Some cultures are thousands of years old and have remained relatively unchanged through time. Others have readily mixed with other peoples and cultures to create new ethnic blends.

There are more than half a billion people in Southeast Asia; nearly half live in Indonesia. The Philippines has more than 84

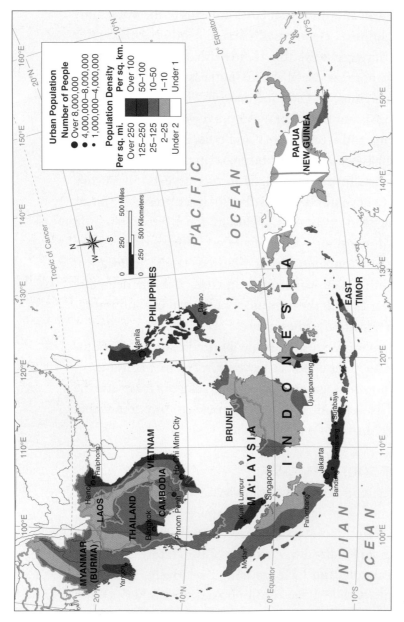

The population density of Southeast Asia varies widely from country to country. For example, Singapore is one of the world's most densely populated countries with 17,500 people per square mile, whereas Laos has only 61 people per square mile.

million people; Vietnam is close behind with more than 80 million. Nearly 65 million people live in Thailand. Brunei is the smallest country in terms of population with fewer than half a million. Within these ten countries is a wide range of human dynamics. For example, the life expectancy is more than 80 years for a person in Singapore but is only in the mid-50s for a person born in Laos, Burma, or Cambodia. The rate of natural population increase (births over deaths) ranges from a high of 1.7 percent per year in Laos to a low 0.7 percent in urban Singapore and in Burma, where the oppressive military regime seems to have toppled people's hope for the future.

According to census data, the population density also varies widely in the region. Singapore is one of the world's most densely populated countries, with more than 17,500 people per square mile; the density in Laos is only 61 in the same area. Singapore's population is 100 percent urban, because the country is a modern "city-state." Laos and Cambodia are the least urban, with only 17 percent and 16 percent, respectively, of the population located in urban areas.

Malaysia is the region's leading car-driving nation, with 424 vehicles per 1,000 people. It is also the country with the most carbon dioxide emissions: 5.2 metric tons per person. Burma has the lowest number of cars per 1,000 people, with only 2.

HIV/AIDS is a growing threat in the region, as it is much of the world. In Laos, it affects 2.7 percent of the population and in Thailand 1.8 percent. The problem is growing rapidly in Thailand, where prostitution is a large-scale business. Hundreds of thousands of young adults are involved in this unsavory activity, which is used to attract many foreign visitors.

Literacy varies widely in the region. Brunei, Singapore, Vietnam, Thailand, and the Philippines boast literacy rates higher than 90 percent, but in Laos only about half of the population can read and write. The literacy rate for males is higher than for females in all Southeast Asian countries. This imbalance is the result of a subtle and obvious bias against females that is evident in many of these cultures, in which males tend to be more highly valued. The literacy rate varies by nearly 30 percent in Laos, where two-thirds of males are literate but only about one-third of all females are. The literacy gender gap is 20 percent in Cambodia, 11 percent in Burma, 8 percent in Indonesia, and 7 percent in Malaysia and Singapore. In Thailand, Vietnam, and the Philippines, the gap drops to less than 3 percent.

People from Southeast Asia have immigrated to virtually all corners of the world. These migrants bring their religions, food, and many other cultural practices as they create a new life and influence the culture into which they have infused themselves. The population of the region is projected to reach nearly 800 million by 2050, thereby ensuring this region's continuing impact on the world. Indonesia is projected to reach 315 million people, Vietnam 132 million, and the Philippines 132 million by midcentury. The most astounding growth is projected for Laos, which is expected to double its population by 2050.

LANGUAGE

Hundreds of different languages and dialects are spoken in Southeast Asia. Some are local indigenous languages such as Vietnamese, Lao, Thai, Burmese, and Khmer. Others are the languages introduced by colonial powers and traders, including English, French, Dutch, Spanish, Chinese, Japanese, and Arabic. Forms of the Malay language are used in not only Malaysia, but also in Brunei, Indonesia, and Singapore.

Historically, three major families of indigenous languages were present in the region before the arrival of outside languages like English, Dutch, French, and Chinese. The three family groups are Austronesian, Austro-Asiatic, and Sino-Tibetan.

The Austronesian languages represent about one-fifth of the world's tongues, with more than 1,200 groupings. This language family includes the primary Malaysian, Philippine, and Indonesian languages. The Austro-Asiatic group is believed to have its roots in southeast China and includes languages like Vietnamese and Khmer, the primary language of Cambodia. Sino-Tibetan languages include Thai, Burmese, and Lao. The Sino-Tibetan language family has more than one billion speakers worldwide. It is a tonal language in which a changing tone alters the meaning of the word. A simple Thai word like *maa*, for example, can mean "horse," "dog," or "to come," depending on the tones used when the word is said. The Austronesian and Austro-Asiatic languages are not tonal.

Colonization by European powers also left a linguistic imprint on the region. French can be found in the former colonies of Cambodia, Laos, and Vietnam, and English is widely used across the region. Spanish is spoken by many Filipinos. The influence of China, both historically and in contemporary society, also has left its languages across the region in places like Singapore, Brunei, Vietnam, and Malaysia.

RELIGION

Many of the religions in Southeast Asia—including Buddhism, Hinduism, Islam, Confucianism, and Christianity—have roots that can be traced back thousands of years. Some, such as Hinduism, Confucianism, and Buddhism, have roots in South Asia. Christianity and Islam came from the Middle East, spread either by Europeans or Arab traders. Some faiths are practiced only by a small number of people in limited areas. Sikhs, for example, are in Malaysia and Singapore, but there is little evidence of them elsewhere.

Local religions abound in the region and include a wide variety of beliefs. One of these is animism. Animism is strong in Laos and other countries where the belief in spirits called *phi* influences the thinking that people have about nature, ancestors, illness, and community. Animism is often tied closely to Buddhism in countries such as Laos, Vietnam, Burma, Thailand, and Cambodia, where ancestors are frequently worshipped. At the same time, many Muslims in Indonesia also incorporate aspects of animism, as do Christians and Hindus in parts of the

RELIGIONS IN SOUTHEAST ASIA

	Buddhist	Christian*	Hindu	Muslim	Indigenous and Other
Brunei	13%	10%	—	67%	10%
Burma	89%	4%	—	4%	3%
Cambodia	95%	—	—	—	5%
Indonesia	1%	8%	2%	88%	1%
Laos	60%	2%	—	—	38%
Malaysia	22%	9%	5%	58%	6%
Philippines	3%	92%	—	5%	—
Singapore	28%	19%	9%	4%	40%
Thailand	94%	1%	—	4%	1%
Vietnam	54%	8%	—	1%	37%

* Includes Roman Catholic and Protestant religions

aspects of animism, as do Christians and Hindus in parts of the region. Usually, animism is practiced in rural rice-growing areas. It is much less common in urban areas, where educated people often consider it to be a belief system based on superstition.

The chart above shows the strength of various religions in the countries of Southeast Asia.

Each of these religions has its own beliefs and story about how it arrived in Southeast Asia. These are explored in the next section of this chapter.

Islam

The world's most populated Islamic country is not in the Middle East but rather is in Southeast Asia. With more than

200 million Muslims, Indonesia is by far the country with the largest number of followers of Islam. This represents the majority of Indonesians: Nearly 88 percent identify themselves as Muslim. Islam in Southeast Asia, however, is a more varied faith than it is in the Middle East. Many different branches of the faith are found throughout the region, and sometimes Islam mixes in with local customs and traditions to form hybrid religions. In Indonesia, for example, a rural Javanese Muslim might go to the mosque to pray and then later also pray at the grave of a local saint. Islam also has reached into the politics of countries in Southeast Asia. In countries such as Indonesia and Malaysia, some of the major religious groups exert a strong influence on political parties and politics.

The prophet Mohammed founded Islam with a belief in monotheism (a single god). Mohammed established the basic tenets of Islam in the faith's holy book called the Koran (or Qu'ran) which was originally written in Arabic. Mohammad lived in Saudi Arabia in the seventh century, and the Koran is a compilation of writings that reflect God's (Allah's) revelations to Mohammad. Today, converts to Islam have spread into Malaysia, Burma, Indonesia, Singapore, and other countries in the region, and across the world

Islam arrived in Southeast Asia between the twelfth and fifteenth centuries. First contact was in Indonesia and on peninsular Malaysia. Later, Islam found its way to the Philippines, Burma, and Thailand. The first form of Islam in Indonesia and Malaysia was Sufi. The word means "wool," the name taken from the practice of early Sufi believers who often wore woolen robes. Converts dedicated themselves to the mystical life known as Sufi, in which believers seek a union with God. Many of these believers combined the new ideas with local traditions and customs. As a result, the roots of Islam in Southeast Asia took on a local flavor.

Muslims believe in the five pillars of Islam, which are the following:

1. Accepting the testimony of faith; Allah is the one true God
2. Praying five times a day: at dawn, noon, midafternoon, sunset, and night
3. Giving alms, or support to the needy
4. Fasting from dawn to sunset during the month of Ramadan
5. Making a pilgrimage to Mecca, Islam's holiest city, at least once during a person's lifetime

Ramadan is conducted in the ninth month of the Islamic calendar, a lunar calendar that is different from the solar calendar used in most of the world. Just before Ramadan, many Muslims visit family gravesites to pay respect to their ancestors. Once Ramadan begins, Muslims stop eating before dawn and fast until sunset. They are also encouraged to refrain from drinking, smoking, lying, anger, cursing, and other bad habits. The time of fasting during the daylight hours is believed to be important for increasing spirituality and developing stronger self-control. After sunset, the family may have a feast with extended family and friends. In modern times, the end of the daily fast is announced on television and a traditional day may end with a meal bought at Kentucky Fried Chicken as the elements of Islam blend with Western businesses. The end of Ramadan is a holiday. Muslims celebrate the occasion with a full-day feast. It also marks the beginning of a time when people visit family and friends to ask for forgiveness for wrongs they have committed during the past year.

Another important Muslim celebration is the *hajj*, in the twelfth lunar month. It is the time when Muslims go to Mecca to circle the black rock called the "Kaaba," Islam's holiest site. Muslims from around the world flock to Mecca for the hajj, which forces Saudi Arabia to limit the number of people who come from different countries. Rahim, a Muslim from Malaysia, made his first trip to Mecca in 2004. He lives in Penang, Malaysia, and is nearing 60 years of age. He and his wife waited years to get permission from Saudi Arabia to make the pilgrimage. Before traveling to Mecca, he shaved his head for this important experience.

In the late twentieth century, Islam started to change in Indonesia and some other areas of Southeast Asia. Many Indonesian workers went to Saudi Arabia in the late 1990s. There, they often connected with a more radical Saudi strain of Islam called *Wahhabism*. This sect of Islam seeks to take the religion back to its fundamental roots as described in the Koran and cleanse it of modern heresies and practices. Proponents of this viewpoint reject habits like smoking, and they forbid gravestones because they consider them idols. Muslim opponents of Wahhabism, often Sufis, contend that it is not true to the Koran and is actually a new form of Islam. Because of this disagreement, proponents of Wahhabism are also predisposed against Sufism. Many followers have become anti-Western because of this extreme belief structure. Recent terrorist acts conducted by Jemaah Islamiyah are connected to the extremist Wahhabis. Today, this group is developing religious schools in Indonesia and other locations; some support Osama bin Laden.

Over time, the conflict has grown between traditional Muslims and the Wahhabis, whose beliefs are more dogmatic and extreme, and it has spilled over into politics. In Indonesia, traditional Muslims are linked to the Nahdlatul Ulama (NU) political party, whereas the Wahhabis support the Muhammadiyah ("the way of Mohammad") party. In Malaysia, the Parti Islam SeMalaysia (Islamic Party of Malaysia, or PAS) is a political party that represents more fundamentalist Islamic viewpoints. In contrast, the Barisan National (National Front, or BN) is a coalition of moderate Muslim parties.

Islam and Buddhism are practiced throughout Southeast Asia. Mosques and temples abound, including the Golden Temple in Bangkok, Thailand, pictured here.

Mosques abound in Malaysia, Indonesia, Brunei, Singapore, and other areas of Southeast Asia where Muslims are located. To Muslims, mosques symbolize eternal tranquility. The third-largest mosque in the world and the largest in Southeast Asia is located in Jakarta, Indonesia. This huge building is called the Istiqlal Great Mosque, and it can hold more than 100,000 people during sermons and prayer. Sadly, this building was bombed in April 1999. Christian extremists were believed to have been responsible; fighting between Christians and Muslims has often taken place in Indonesia. Other important mosques in Southeast Asia include the National Mosque in Kuala Lumpur, Malaysia and Brunei's famous gold-domed floating mosque called Omar Ali Saifuddien. Even Singapore, with only 18 percent of the population Muslim, has more than 70 mosques. Islam, like Christianity, is not a monolithic faith in which everyone believes in the same traditions and practices in the same way. Many varieties are evident in Southeast Asia.

Buddhism

Many people in Southeast Asia practice Buddhism, a faith that began in India and found a home in this region. Buddhism, in fact, is the dominant religion in Burma, Thailand, Cambodia, Laos, and Vietnam. Buddhism also has many followers in Brunei, Singapore, and Malaysia, with a presence also in the Philippines and Indonesia. With its broad distribution across each of the countries in Southeast Asia, Buddhism touches the region in a way that no other religion does.

Buddhism got its start with Siddhartha Gautama, an Indian prince of the warrior class who was raised in a wealthy family around the sixth century B.C. His childhood in a palace was very comfortable and sheltered, and he had little exposure to the harsh realities of the outside world. He became uncomfortable with his life of luxury and started to travel outside of his protected palace in search of enlightenment. He was shocked to find that disease, poverty, misery, and death lay just beyond the palace gates. These observations first led him to a life of auster-ity: He ate little and searched for wisdom. After seven years, this path was not satisfying his quest for deeper understanding, so he began to seek what he referred to as the middle path, a road between greedy self-indulgence and total austerity.

In Sarnath, India, Siddhartha Gautama became enlight-ened. His enlightenment led him to advocate an ethical doctrine that sought to liberate people from suffering by hav-ing them achieve higher states of consciousness. Soon, people began to refer to him as "Buddha," which means "enlight-ened one."

Buddhism is an ethical code of living and philosophy rather than a religion in the manner of Christianity or Islam. Buddha believed that the search for material things caused only suffer-ing. This suffering causes a person to be reborn into another life that is again marked by suffering. Buddha taught that people should cast out worldly desires. If they did so, they would not need to be reborn into another life of suffering. Buddha called the state where rebirth was not necessary "nirvana." To achieve nirvana, Buddha advocated an Eightfold Path that teaches fol-lowers to believe right, desire right, think right, live right, do the right things, think the right thoughts, behave right, and practice deep reflection.

Buddhism is a strong presence in Southeast Asia, and this has affected daily life in that most believe in nonviolence. Bud-dhists usually worship in their own homes. They often have statues of Buddha in their homes because the faith is often prac-ticed by maintaining the five precepts or promises. These pre-cepts are as follows:

1. Not to harm or kill any living things
2. Not to steal or take anything that is not freely given
3. To control sexual desires
4. Not to tell lies
5. Not to drink or take drugs

Although many Buddhists worship at home, there are many fabulous temples such as Angkor Wat in Cambodia. Angkor Wat is the work of Suryavarman II (A.D. 1113–1150). *Wat* is the Khmer word for *temple*.

Buddhists often worship at home, but they also have built many fantastic temples in Southeast Asia, with thousands of statues, large and small, of Buddha. In Bangkok, Thailand, there is the Temple of the Emerald Buddha in the Grand Palace, and at the Wat Traimit there is a solid gold Buddha that stands nearly ten feet high and weighs five and a half tons. The Kek Lok Si Temple, in Penang, Malaysia, is the largest in Southeast Asia. Other important Buddhist temples include Borobudur in Indonesia, Angkor Wat in Cambodia, Shwe Dagon Pagoda in Burma, and the Wat Xieng Thong Temple, where kings were once crowned in Laos.

Christianity

Small numbers of Christians are scattered across Southeast Asia. Only in the Philippines, where 83 percent of the population is Roman Catholic, is Christianity the dominant faith. Protestant churches, including Baptist, Methodist, Lutheran, the Church of Latter-Day Saints, and others, are also evident in Southeast Asia. Many of these Christian churches came with early European explorers who colonized areas in the region and converted locals to Christianity.

Christianity in the Philippines is much like Islam in Indonesia. The local population has combined many traditional aspects of animism with the newer religions. Spaniards introduced Christianity to the islands in 1565, when they established the first Spanish settlement on the island of Cebu. The new faith began to challenge the influence of Islam, which had arrived a century earlier. Many local people adopted Catholicism by superimposing it over their older traditional beliefs. This process led to a form of Christianity in the Philippines that is somewhat different from Christianity elsewhere.

Catholics and other Christians hold the Bible as their most holy book. They believe that Jesus Christ is the son of God and died for the sins of believers. The Ten Commandments, along with the teachings of Jesus that are contained in the New Testament of the Bible, present fundamental beliefs for Christians. Emphasis is placed on loving one another, prayer, and reading the Bible. Christmas, a celebration of Christ's birth, and Easter, which represents the resurrection of Christ, are two important Christian holidays. In the Philippines, a fiesta has been added as a local religious celebration in which a social event is build around a special Mass or church service. Related fiesta activities may include basketball tournaments, cockfights, a carnival, and other competitions. The local fiestas serve to bring the community together in a religiously inspired gathering.

Religion plays an important role in the lives of many people in Southeast Asia, and many hold religious beliefs other than those discussed in this chapter. Hinduism is practiced by some in Malaysia, Indonesia, Singapore, and Thailand. More obscure religions, such as Hoa Hao and Cao Dai, are practiced in Vietnam, and other local belief systems are practiced elsewhere in the region.

THE ARTS

Song, dance, literature, theater, and other arts abound in Southeast Asia. Variations of the *wayang,* or Chinese opera, are performed in many parts of the region, including Singapore, Indonesia, Thailand, Malaysia, Brunei, and the Philippines. In the wayang, shadow puppets tell a traditional story that often has Indian roots in the Hindu Ramayana. The puppets, used for showing and telling the story, can be very elaborate and ornate.

Traditional Balinese, Cambodian, Lao, Thai, and other dances are very graceful. Intricate hand movements are performed by the dancers, who are clad in colorful costumes often ornamented with gold and rich colors that vary by region. The heads of dancers are covered by crowns that are artistically decorated. Women who perform Thai fawn dances wear six-inch-long brass nails that accentuate the choreographed hand movements that are in classical harmony with the music and dance steps. The accompanying instruments usually include some form of percussion and flutelike woodwinds.

Art in the region tends to be a reflection of life. Bold and impressive religious expressions are found in art, sculpture, and architecture of Southeast Asia. Bronze sculptures, Thai crowns, gilded Buddha statues, Indonesian masks, and artistic *batik* clothing are but a few examples of the art forms that exist in the region.

FOOD

Southeast Asia has been known as a region of spices for hundreds of years. Indonesia was once called the Spice Islands because of the rare flavorings found in the archipelago. Regional foods reflect the richness and variety that a visitor would expect. Spices used to flavor foods include nutmeg, cloves, pepper, and coriander. Mint leaf, garlic, green onion, coconut milk, and a wide variety of other indigenous and imported items are also used. Outside influences are evident in regional foods—the Chinese, Spanish, Indian, French, and even the Portuguese (who brought the chili pepper from the Americas) have contributed to the taste sensations now found in the region.

In addition to the wonderful variety and taste of food in Southeast Asia, great pride is taken in visual presentation. Meals usually include a mixture of flavors and textures such as sweet, salty, and bitter. Rice is included as a staple in most Southeast Asian diets. Noodles are served occasionally, particularly in areas influenced by the Chinese. In most of the region, meals are served all at once rather than as a sequence of courses, with the exception of dessert. Dessert is usually a selection of local fruits, picked at the peak of ripeness, instead of the sweet pastry desserts found in the West. Most people in the region eat with their right hands or with spoons, knives, and forks. Vietnam is the exception to this: The Chinese have had greater influence here, and so chopsticks are commonly used.

History has shown that it can be very difficult to effectively govern countries within a region of such tremendous cultural diversity. In the next chapter, you will learn how culture can affect government and how the region continues to search for ever-elusive political stability.

CHAPTER 6

Political Geography

In a democracy, governments ruled by the people help bring structure and popular support for the ruling parties elected to leadership. In dictatorships, rule is by a select few individuals or a small
party, like the Communist Party, that governs in a totalitarian (au-
thoritarian) manner. Dictatorships can be harsh or benevolent depending on the character of the leaders. In dictatorships, the rule of
one or more individuals prevails over the rule of law that is found in
democratic governments. Rule of law is a vitally important idea in
democracies: It means that no person is above the law. Even leaders
are subject to the law and to punishment if they violate the laws of the
society. Monarchy is another form of government, one in which a
ruling family presides over the government. Rule in this society is

STATUS OF GOVERNMENT IN THE VARIOUS COUNTRIES OF SOUTHEAST ASIA

	Year of Present Constitution*	Type of Government	Head of State	Head of Government	Legislative Branch	Names of Houses	Highest Court
Brunei	1959	Malay Islamic monarchy	Sultan	Sultan	Laws are made by royal proclamation	Fve councils advise the sultan	High Court
Cambodia	1993	Democracy under a constitutional monarchy	King	Prime minister	Bicameral	National Assembly and Senate	Supreme Court and Supreme Council of the Magistracy
Indonesia	1945	Republic	President	President	Unicameral	Dewan Perwakilan Rakyat (DPR)	Supreme Court
Laos	1991	Communist state	President	Prime minister	Unicameral	National Assembly	People's Supreme Court
Malaysia	1957	Constitutional monarchy	Paramount ruler	Prime minister	Bicameral	Dewan Negara and Dewan Rakyat	Federal Court
Myanmar	1974	Military dictatorship	Military prime minister	Military prime minister	Unicameral	People's Assembly (suspended)	No independent courts
Philippines	1987	Republic	President	President	Bicameral	Senate and House of Representatives	Supreme Court
Singapore	1959	Parliamentary republic	President	Prime minister	Unicameral	Parliament	Supreme Court
Thailand	1997	Constitutional monarchy	King	Prime minister	Bicameral	Senate and House of Representatives	Supreme Court
Vietnam	1992	Communist state	President	Prime minister	Unicameral	National Assembly	Supreme People's Court

passed from one generation to the next as kings, queens, sultans, emperors, and empresses inherit the throne from their predecessors. Today, all of these types of government are present in one or more countries throughout the region of Southeast Asia.

Types of government within the region range from military dictatorship in Myanmar (Burma) to historical monarchies in Thailand and Brunei. The Philippines is a democratic state. Between those three forms of government are places like Thailand and Malaysia, which are constitutional monarchies, and Brunei, which is a constitutional sultanate.

Since the end of World War II, there has been a slow trend toward democratic government. Indonesia, Singapore, Malaysia, Cambodia, and the Philippines have made major moves toward democratic governments. Unfortunately, however, this does not mean that citizens are fully afforded all of the rights and freedoms as advocated by the United Nations Declaration of Human Rights.

Each of the countries in Southeast Asia has its own political story to tell. The range of structures and institutions in these countries is great. In some places, the people have no power; in others, they have a very strong voice. A brief survey of the countries and their political context is a story worth telling in that it provides a backdrop for understanding the countries and their relationships with others.

SURVEY OF GOVERNMENT BY COUNTRY
Brunei Darussalam

Brunei had been under British rule for more than a century when the Japanese occupied it during World War II. The Australians liberated Brunei at the end of the war and returned the area to the British. Finally, in 1984, Brunei achieved full independence. The sultan became prime minister.

Brunei gave supreme authority to the sultan in the 1959 constitution, which was suspended in 1962 after an attempted

Brunei's Sultan Hassanal Bolkiah prays with Queen Mariam Haji Abdul Aziz during his 54th birthday celebration at Nurul Iman (State) Palace in Bandar Seri Begawan, capital of Brunei, in this picture taken July 15, 2000. The royal couple announced on February 4, 2003, that they would divorce.

revolution. Since that time, the sultan has ruled by decree, meaning that an order by the sultan has the power of law. The sultan receives advice from five primary councils that are designated in the constitution. These are the Religious Council, the Privy Council, the Council of Ministers, the Legislative Council, and the Council of Succession. The Council of Ministers serves as the Cabinet. From 1959 until 1984, the British conducted the foreign affairs of Brunei and were responsible for its protection. Brunei became fully independent in 1984, and the sultan has ruled by decree since that time.

The sultan stated in 1989 that he would consider liberaliz-
ing Brunei's government if the people showed the potential to
govern in a more democratic government. A government commission investigated this possibility in 1994, but more than a
decade later, the results of the commission have not been released. Because of the relative prosperity of the people from oil
revenues, there has been no significant political opposition to
the rule of the sultan since independence.

Cambodia

The Kingdom of Cambodia fought for and achieved independence from France in 1953, and its story has been violent and tu-
multuous since then. Like the rest of Indochina, Cambodia was
occupied by Japan during World War II until the French re-
gained power in 1945. In the 1960s, the fierce military struggle
in neighboring Vietnam bled over into Cambodia. Then, in
1970, royal Prince Sihanouk was thrown out of power in a military coup. After the coup, the country fell into the hands of the
Khmer Rouge Cambodian Communists. Three million people
are estimated to have died under the rule of the Khmer Rouge.
Many more people fled to Thailand for safety during this era of
horror. In 1978, Vietnam invaded. In 1989, Vietnam withdrew
from Cambodia and Prince Sihanouk again rose to power to
forge political agreements with warring factions and to develop
a more democratic framework for a new government. After the
new constitution was created in 1993, Prince Sihanouk became
king and the last remnants of the Khmer Rouge were finally
eliminated or surrendered. After all the years of civil war and violence, Cambodia was finally able to turn toward more effective
self-rule in the early years of the twenty-first century.

Cambodia's government consists of three branches and is a
constitutional monarchy, with Prince Sihanouk as the
monarch. The king serves as the chief of state, but the position
is not hereditary; rather, it is appointed by the Royal Throne
Council. The Executive Branch is headed by the prime minister,

who is a member of the ruling political party or ruling coalition. The Legislative Branch consists of a bicameral (two-housed) legislature. The houses include the National Assembly, with 122 members, and the Senate, with 61 members. The Judicial Branch has the Supreme Court as the highest in the country. Another court, the Supreme Council of the Magistracy, assists in keeping the courts truly independent.

Indonesia

The recent political roots of Indonesia's government lie with the Dutch and also in Japan's wartime occupation of the country. With independence in 1945, Indonesia's constitution established three branches of government that were based on five key elements advocated by Indonesia's first president, Sukarno. They were called the five principles of Pancasila. The elements of Pancasila included God, humanitarianism, national unity, democracy, and social justice.

Indonesia's Executive Branch is led by the president, who is elected by a popular vote of the people. The constitution provides for a strong presidency, and occasionally leaders have abused these powers. Indonesia has a unicameral (one-house) Legislative Branch, called the Dewan Perwakilan Rakyat (DPR). This can be translated to mean "People's Representative Council." The Judicial Branch has the Supreme Court as the highest court, and it also has a special Constitutional Court that has the power to interpret the Constitution.

Indonesia also has two other bodies that meet periodically. One is the Dewan Perwakilan Daerah (DPD), a body of regional representatives. The other body is the Majelis Permusyawaratan Rakyat (MPR), or People's Consultative Assembly, which meets every five years to consider amending the constitution. Neither is truly a legislative body; each has very specific constitutional responsibilities.

A challenge that faces Indonesia is that the thousands of islands and many sharp cultural differences, including language and religion, make it difficult to govern. Separatist movements and extremist groups affiliated with al Qaeda have operated violently in the country and make governance more difficult.

Laos

Laos is one of the world's few remaining Communist states. Independence was gained in 1949, and, like Cambodia and Vietnam, Laos has historical roots in French Indochina. The Lao People's Revolutionary Party is the name for the Communists, and the party completely dominates the political structure. A new constitution was adopted in 1991; under it, three branches of government were established. The Executive Branch is led by the president, who serves as the chief of state, and the prime minister, who is the head of the government.

Laos has a unicameral legislature called the National Assembly that has 109 members. The People's Supreme Court is the highest court in the country, and members are elected by the National Assembly. The country has started to become more involved with its neighbors and was admitted as a member of ASEAN in 1997.

Malaysia

Malaysia was formed in 1963 as a federation of various British colonies in the region that included Malaya, Sabah, Sarawak, and Singapore. Singapore withdrew from the new country in 1965 and declared its independence. The government is a constitutional monarchy. It operates with a monarch called the paramount ruler, who is elected for a five-year term by the hereditary rulers of nine of Malaysia's states. The paramount ruler serves as the chief of state, and the prime minister serves as the head of the government. The prime minister is usually the leader of the majority group or party in Malaysia's House of Representatives. The progressive, but often controversial, Mahathir bin Mohammed served as prime minister from 1981 until he stepped down in the fall of 2003 after making a number of anti-Semitic comments at an international gathering of Islamic leaders.

Malaysia's bicameral parliament represents the country's legislative branch. The Senate, or Dewan Negara, has 69 members; 43 of these members are appointed by the paramount ruler, and the other 26 are appointed by the state legislatures. The House of Representatives, or Dewan Rakyat, has 219 members, who are elected by popular vote for terms of five years. The Federal Court is the highest court in Malaysia, and the members are appointed by the paramount ruler with the counsel of the prime minister.

Burma

Burma gained its independence from the British in 1948. Democratic foundations were established in the early years after independence, but these were smashed when General Ne Win overthrew the government and established single-party socialist rule. The general ruled until 1988, when demonstrations drove him from power. Later in 1988, the military again seized control. In 1990, elections were held and an opposition party called the National League for Democracy, led by Aung San Suu Kyi, won an overwhelming victory. The election results were quashed by the military leaders, however, and the newly elected leaders were placed under house arrest.

Today, there is great interest on the part of citizens in having civilian rule restored in Burma. Aung San Suu Kyi was jailed until 2002, but she has remained in the forefront of the antimilitary political movement. In 1991, she received one of the world's highest honors, the coveted Nobel Peace Prize, for her efforts to advance democracy. The country's constitution has been suspended since 1988. Work began on a new constitution in 1993, but as of 2005, it had not been released to the citizenry. Thus, Burma remains a military dictatorship where dissidents are routinely jailed and few freedoms exist for citizens.

During elections, political posters dominate the scenery. This photo was taken near Penang, Malaysia, in Prime Minister Abdullah's home area on election day.

The Philippines

The Philippines had two colonial masters before World War II. The United States gained control of the Philippines in 1898, after the Spanish-American War. With this American connection, the Philippines adopted a constitution that is very similar to that of the United States. This shows the American legacy in the political development of the Philippines, which became independent in 1946 after being occupied by Japan during World War II.

The first three presidents of the Philippines were elected democratically. In 1970, however, then-President Ferdinand Marcos was fighting numerous insurgencies. Trying to end these rebellions and the fighting, he declared martial law in 1972 and adopted a new constitution in 1973. Unfortunately, the new constitution was not democratic and it gave nearly unlimited powers to Marcos. At the same time his wife,

Here, officials are counting votes in Malaysia. Southeast Asia has a history of troubled elections. For instance, the 1986 elections in the Philippines were believed to have been rigged, and in Burma, the 1990 election results were quashed by the military leaders and the elected leaders placed under house arrest.

Imelda, was accumulating political power. Finally, in 1981, Marcos ended the martial law and was reelected to another six-year term.

Politics began to change in the Philippines when Benigno Aquino, an important leader of the political opposition, was assassinated in 1983. This assassination caused political opposition to Marcos to increase. In 1986, Marcos was reelected again, but many believed that the elections were corrupt and unfair. In the belief that the election results had been rigged, opposition leader Corazon Aquino, widow of Benigno, declared herself the winner. Political unrest was at the boiling point, and tens of thousands of people poured out into the streets of Manila and other cities to demonstrate against the continuing rule of Marcos. Pushed to the limit by the protests, Marcos and his wife were forced to flee the country in 1986. Corazon Aquino assumed the presidency and established a new constitution. This constitution was put into place in 1987 and provided for a more democratic government. President Aquino did not run for re-election in 1992, and democratic elections have taken place since 1986.

The constitution provides for a president who serves as the chief of state and the head of the government. Both the president and vice president are elected for six-year terms on separate ballots, which means that they can be from different political parties. This situation can create many political problems in developing and implementing public policies.

The Philippines legislative branch consists of a Congress made up of two houses, the House and the Senate. The Philippine terms for these bodies are the Senado and the Kapulungan Ng Mga Kinatawan. The Senate has only 24 members, who are elected for six-year terms. Half of the Senate is elected every three years. The House has 214 elected members, who serve three-year terms. The president may appoint additional members to the House, but there is a constitutional limit of 250 seats. The highest court in the Judicial Branch is the Supreme Court; members are appointed by the president and may serve until age 70.

Singapore

Singapore is perhaps best known for its unusual laws. In 1994, a young man from the United States gained wide publicity when he was caned for vandalism. Other laws prohibit gum, littering, firecrackers, firearms, and smoking in public. During one recent year, more than 400 people were fined a minimum of $500 (U.S.) for smoking in prohibited places. Littering can bring a fine and public embarrassment: Law breakers' pictures appear in the newspaper or they are forced to wear a bright yellow jacket that says, "I stepped outside of the law." A person can receive the death penalty for having drugs or bringing firearms into Singapore. Failure to flush a public toilet after use can bring a first-time offender a fine of $250. All of these laws are designed to keep Singapore clean, and the laws are viewed very favorably by most citizens.

Singapore has a strong British heritage in its political institutions, even though the colony was occupied by Japan during World War II and was united with Malaysia for a short period of time. Its Legislative Branch, like the United Kingdom's, is called a parliament; it has 84 members, who are elected for a five-year term. Singapore's parliament has one major difference in that it has only one house, as designated by the 1965 constitution. Some important elements of the constitution predate Singapore's independence in 1965: Although it broke away from Malaysia, Singapore chose to retain certain parts of the Malaysian constitution.

The prime minister is the head of government, and Singapore's president is the chief of state. The president is elected in a popular vote for a six-year term. The prime minister is appointed by the president and is usually the head of the majority party or ruling coalition. The Supreme Court is the highest court in Singapore, with members appointed by the president.

Thailand

Thailand is a constitutional monarchy, which means that it is democratically ruled but by a king. The monarchy in Thailand is hereditary, and the king serves as the chief of state. A prime minister, who is appointed by the king from the ruling party or coalition, serves as the head of the government. By tradition, the prime minister is usually the head of the majority party or coalition in the House of Representatives (Sapha Phuthaen Ratsadon). The House has 500 members. The other body in Thailand's bicameral National Assembly is the 200-seat Senate

(Wuthisapha). Members of both houses are elected by popular vote for four-year terms. The highest court is the Supreme Court, or Sandika, which has judges appointed by the king.

Vietnam

The Socialist Republic of Vietnam, like Laos, is one of the few remaining Communist states. Its 1992 constitution designated the president as the chief of state and the prime minister as the head of government in the Executive Branch. The president is selected by the unicameral National Assembly for a five-year term. The president selects the prime minister.

The Communist Party of Vietnam (CPV) essentially runs the government because it is the only political party. Other candidates can run for the National Assembly, but only with the approval of the CPV. The National Assembly has 498 seats filled by popular vote, and members are elected for five-year terms. Normally more than 90 percent of the seats are filled by the CPV, and the others are held by CPV-approved candidates. The Supreme People's Court serves as the highest court in the Judicial Branch, which retains some of its French colonial traditions in civil matters. Many problems exist for citizens, who have few political rights and freedoms, and the courts are not completely independent of the political pressure of the CPV. Dissent is nonexistent, and disagreements from citizens are quashed by the power of the state and the CPV.

Southeast Asia has a remarkable array of political systems that have been examined in the preceding section. What are the rights and freedoms of citizens? How do they vary across the region and what problems exist?

CITIZEN RIGHTS IN SOUTHEAST ASIA

Certain basic rights have been established by the international community. These serve as a baseline for countries to draw on when developing their constitution and laws. The UN's Declaration of Human Rights is a primary tool that can be used to

	Freedom or Right of Expression	Religion	Assembly/ Association	Privacy	Movement	Own Property	Fair Trial	Equality	Press Media
Brunei*	no	no[‡,§]	no[§]	no	no	no	no[‡]	no	no[‡,§]
Burma[†]	no[‡,§]	no[§]	no[‡,§]	no[§]	no[§]	no[§]	no[‡,§]	no[§]	no[§]
Cambodia	yes	yes	yes	yes	yes	yes	yes[‡]	yes[‡]	yes
Indonesia	yes	yes	yes	implied	yes	yes	no[‡]	yes	yes[‡]
Laos	yes[‡]	yes[‡]	yes[‡]	no	no	no	no[‡]	yes	yes
Malaysia	yes	yes[‡]	yes[‡]	no	no	yes	yes	yes	no
Philippines	yes	yes	yes	yes	yes	yes	yes[‡]	yes	yes
Singapore	yes[‡]	yes[‡]	yes[‡]	no	yes	yes	yes	yes	no
Thailand	yes[‡]	yes	yes	yes	yes	yes	yes[§]	yes	yes[‡]
Vietnam	yes[‡,§]	yes[‡,§]	yes[‡,§]	yes[§]	yes[§]	yes	yes[§]	yes[‡]	yes[§]

* Constitution of Brunei has suspended freedoms and rights since 1962
[†] Burma is ruled by a military regime who rules by decree in absence of a promised constitution
[‡] Concerns indicated by Amnesty International
[§] Concerns indicated by the U.S. State Department

examine fundamental rights and freedoms that can be expected for citizens. The chart above indicates many of the rights stated in the Declaration of Human Rights and outlines how the countries in Southeast Asia match up in these areas.

It is evident that citizens in some countries have few, if any, meaningful freedoms. Even relatively free nations such as Singapore have strict censorship of the media. In the past, publications like *Newsweek* and *Time* have been excluded because they have published articles critical of Singapore's political leadership.

Other basic rights such as freedom of movement are not guaranteed in the constitutions of four Southeast Asian nations. This means that citizens may not be permitted to move to another community to be near relatives or to locate a job.

Some countries state in their constitutions that a particular right or freedom is protected, but in reality the practice is severely restricted. An example of this widespread policy can be drawn from Vietnam. Article 69 of Vietnam's constitution states, "The citizen shall enjoy freedom of opinion and speech, freedom of the press, the right to be informed, and the right to assemble, form associations and hold demonstrations in accordance with the provisions of the law." Even with this clear wording, both the United States State Department and Amnesty International have expressed concerns with the actual implementation of these freedoms and cite abuses that have taken place in recent years.

FOREIGN RELATIONS

Most countries in Southeast Asia are actively engaged in the international community. Some countries, such as Burma, are more limited in their foreign relations because of the political repression that has been practiced by the ruling military junta (ruling group, often one that seizes power after a coup). Working to enforce international norms, bodies like the United Nations and other organizations may impose penalties or sanctions on regimes that do not comply with international standards. The result of such actions is that non-complying countries become even more isolated from the global community.

Along with membership in international organizations, many countries have agreed to major international treaties. All of the ten Southeast Asian nations have signed on to the Nuclear Nonproliferation Treaty and the Montreal Protocol on Substances That Deplete the Ozone Layer. All of the countries in the region, except Brunei, have also signed on to the Kyoto Protocol, an international agreement that strives to limit greenhouse gas emissions on the planet. In late 2003, the Philippines, Malaysia, Singapore, and Indonesia supplied personnel to various United Nation peacekeeping efforts around the world. As is evident from the chart and the other information provided here, the countries in Southeast Asia are actively involved in the international community. This involvement has been increasing in recent years and is a factor that contributes to the growth of democracies in the region.

Democracy has been on the rise in Southeast Asia since the second half of the twentieth century. Most were colonies of European powers that finally achieved independence after World War II. Most of these colonies also suffered greatly under Japanese occupation. Some of the newly independent countries, such as the Philippines, Indonesia, and Thailand, struggled with dictatorial leaders or the military. Others, including Laos, Cambodia, and Vietnam, have a recent Communist heritage that makes the transition to a democratic government slower. Many countries that have moved politically toward more democratic governments have found economic prosperity as a side benefit. This has happened in Singapore, Malaysia, and other nations where there is less government control of the economy. More change may be ahead as the threat of terrorism persists in some of the democracies and as citizens demand more freedoms in dictatorships like Burma. Most likely, the governments of Southeast Asia will remain in a state of evolution and transition during at least the early decades of the twenty-first century.

CHAPTER 7

Economic Geography

Tremendous changes have occurred in the economies of Southeast Asia since the end of World War II. After gaining independence after the war, the new Southeast Asian countries took their economies into their own hands and began the difficult process of building noncolonial economies. This process started slowly for many countries but was aided in 1967, with the formation of the Association of Southeast Asian Nations, or ASEAN. In Vietnam and Cambodia, the process took place later; the ravages of war and the folly of centrally controlled economies delayed development until the 1980s. Burma, afflicted by military rule and external economic sanctions, is developing slowly even today, as a full

A little girl plays with a computer at a computer shop in Kuala Lampur, November 5, 2000. The Malaysian government recently urged Malaysian people to have at least one computer in each home so that they can acquire more knowledge of information technology.

member of ASEAN. For some countries, such as Malaysia, Thailand, and Singapore, the economic development in recent decades has been astounding.

Some countries have developed expertise in modern technology that places them among the world's leaders in terms of computer hardware and access. A major part of this transition has been the move from agriculture to service and high-tech-based economies in countries such as Malaysia and Singapore. Some countries remain tied to agricultural production because government limitations have impeded the development

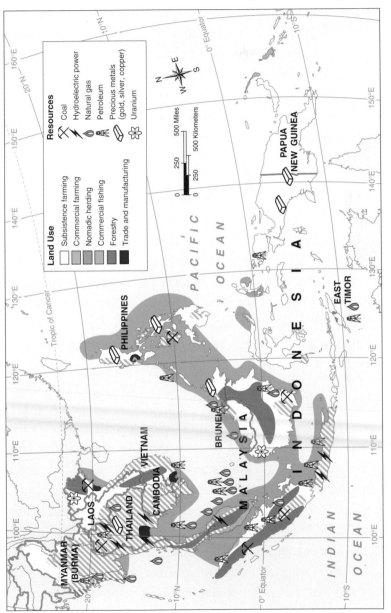

The economic development of Southeast Asia has changed dramatically since the end of World War II from an agricultural economy to a service and high-technology economy. Natural resources, such as gas and oil, are also very important to this region's economy, particularly in Brunei and Burma.

of free-market systems that have been successful in other countries in the region. Countries such as Vietnam, Cambodia, Laos, and Burma fall into this latter category, whereas Indonesia and the Philippines are following a more traditional blend of agriculture, industrialization, and services in their path to economic development. The economy of Brunei falls into another category because the economy has depended on the production and exportation of oil and natural gas. A brief survey of the individual economies is a way of quickly looking at key elements in each.

BRUNEI

Brunei is extremely dependent on the oil and gas industry and has almost no other significant exports. Oil production has declined since 1979, but the small country still is the third-largest producer of oil in Southeast Asia and the fourth-largest producer of natural gas in the world. Half of Brunei's exported oil goes to Japan; the United States, Korea, Thailand, and Taiwan are also major trade destinations. Brunei is projected to have oil supplies to last until 2015, and the country is hoping that deep-sea exploration will identify new fields.

BURMA

Burma is a country rich in natural resources. Petroleum, natural gas, coal deposits, and hydroelectric development provide rich stores of energy. Metals include tin, antimony, zinc, copper, tungsten, and lead. The country also produces marble and precious stones and has vast expanses of forest that supply timber. Currently, only natural gas is being exploited at its full potential in this military-controlled country. Other resources are developed poorly, if at all. Haphazard economic leadership has kept most of the rural population living in poverty. Nearly 70 percent of the country's population is engaged in subsistence agriculture; very few farmers raise crops for export. Exports include small amounts of rice and beans. Unofficial black market trade and illegal drugs are believed to account for a significant, although undocumented, part of the economy.

CAMBODIA

Until 1999, Cambodia was torn by three decades of war. The fighting, which took more than one million lives, kept the population in a state of terror and the economy at a standstill. Since the end of the fighting, the economy has grown at a healthy annual rate, averaging more than 5 percent. The country is beset by many problems, however: Low literacy rates, the possibility of resumed military conflict, and rampant corruption have combined to keep foreign parties wary of investing in Cambodia. Tourism was the most rapidly gaining industry since 1999, but it was heavily impacted by the September 11, 2001, terrorist attacks on the United States. More than one-third of the population lives below the poverty level. About 80 percent of the population is engaged in agriculture, producing mainly rice, corn, and vegetables, as well as rubber. Most exports go to the United States; Germany, Japan, and the United Kingdom are other recipients of Cambodian goods.

INDONESIA

The largest and most populated country in Southeast Asia is Indonesia. Indonesia has a long and well-chronicled history of trade with other lands. Today, major trading partners include Japan, the United States, South Korea, China, and Singapore. Currently, the economy is mixed. Most Indonesians still work in agriculture, but manufacturing and service sectors of the economy are experiencing rapid growth. As of 2004, only 16 percent of the population was engaged in manufacturing, but this group is responsible for 44 percent of the country's gross domestic product (GDP). At the same time, 45 percent of the work force is engaged in agriculture, but the sector only generates 17 percent of Indonesia's GDP.

With labor costs low, it would seem likely that more foreign investors would flock to the country to start new industries and create jobs. Many problems face the country, however, and potential investors are very wary of risking their capital. Corruption is rampant, religious conflict is widespread, and the country is experiencing several often-violent separatist movements. It also suffers from a weak banking system, a variety of security issues including a number of terrorist cells, and strained relations with the International Monetary Fund (IMF).

Indonesia does have some strong advantages that favor economic growth. It has huge stores of oil and natural gas, and development of these fuel resources leads the manufacturing sector in the economy. Japan is the primary market for these exports. Other natural resources in Indonesia's chest of riches include tin, nickel, bauxite, and copper, as well as deposits of gold and silver. The country also has fertile soils, and agricultural crops are important to the economy. Rice, the chief staple in the Indonesian diet, is the major crop. Other food crops include peanuts, cocoa, cassava, soybeans, sweet potatoes, corn, and vegetables. Coffee and tobacco are produced, as are tree crops such as palm oil, coconuts, and rubber. Nutmeg, cloves, and black pepper support an important spice trade, as they have for centuries.

Because of its spectacular scenery, beautiful tropical beaches, and fascinating cultures, Indonesia has a tremendous potential to develop a world-class tourist industry. The threat of terrorism, inadequate tourist facilities in many places, and the omnipresent threat of natural disasters tend to discourage further development of this economic sector.

LAOS

As a Communist country, Laos, like China, has made major efforts to decentralize its economy and support privatization. Change has been slow, however, and 80 percent of the population is still engaged in subsistence agriculture. Major agricultural products include food crops such as rice, sweet potatoes, vegetables, corn, and peanuts. Coffee and tea are grown, as is sugarcane. Other crops include tobacco and cotton. Livestock include water buffalo, pigs, and cattle. Laos is a landlocked country, so trade with the wider world is difficult. The country's most important trading partners are neighboring Thailand and Vietnam. Manufactured goods and petroleum make up most of the country's imports. The country also lacks a strong infrastructure of roads, rail, and telecommunications, a factor that hampers extensive rapid economic development. About 40 percent of the population lives in poverty.

MALAYSIA

During recent decades, a strong and responsible democratic government has contributed to a tremendous forward leap in Malaysia's economic development. At the turn of the millennium, Malaysia could boast of having the world's tallest building—the Petronas Twin Towers—a fitting symbol of the country's soaring economy. In the early 1970s, Malaysia was a relatively poor country that produced mainly natural resources. Since that time, it has blossomed into a diversified market economy with many strengths, including well-developed electronics and information technologies. Other important exports include petroleum and liquefied natural gas, wood and wood products, palm oil, rubber, textiles, and chemicals. Japan and the United States are major markets for Malaysia's exports, as are Singapore, Hong Kong, China, and Taiwan. Situated on the strategic Strait of Malacca, Malaysia is well positioned for sea trade.

Malaysians have benefited greatly from their country's economic growth. The country has a booming economy that supports low unemployment and relatively high incomes. Citizens now enjoy a quality of life that is one of the highest in the region. Malaysia is culturally diverse but enjoys ethnic and religious harmony. This factor contributes to the stability and trustworthiness that are essential for attracting foreign companies and other capital investments.

THE PHILIPPINES

This island country faces some of the same difficulties as Indonesia, with separatist movements and a very large public debt. The economy is fairly diverse: Agriculture, light industries, and a strong service sector all contribute. Poverty, however, is a large problem. About 40 percent of the population lives below the poverty level, and unemployment is high, at about 10 percent. Major agricultural products include rice, coconuts, corn, sugarcane, bananas, pineapples, and mangoes. Pork, beef, and eggs also are produced. Major manufacturing products include textiles, pharmaceuticals, chemicals, wood products, food processing, electronics assembly, petroleum refining, and fishing.

The Philippines exports mainly to the United States, Japan, Singapore, South Korea, and Taiwan. Major products include electronic equipment, machinery, transport equipment, garments, coconut products, and chemicals. The country is now attempting to privatize more of the economy in an effort to stimulate growth and to increase trade within the region.

SINGAPORE

This city-state boasts of being the world's second-busiest seaport. Only Rotterdam in the Netherlands is more active. Obviously, this means that trade is an overwhelming factor in Singapore's economy. Lacking any meaningful natural resources, Singapore must rely on its location and ingenuity to develop its economy. Situated at the southern tip of the Malay Peninsula, the country possesses a key location for world trade. To its benefit, free trade has been a mainstay of the island country since

Sir Thomas Stamford Raffles established a British trading post there in 1819.

The citizens of Singapore enjoy high wages, good jobs, and low unemployment because the market economy and political stability have created an outstanding environment for businesses to operate effectively. Food products, petroleum, and other natural resources are major imports. Machinery, equipment, electronics, consumer goods, and chemicals are major exports. Key trading partners include other ASEAN nations, notably Malaysia, as well as the United States and China. Besides being an important shipping port, Singapore is also Southeast Asia's major hub for international air transportation. Many airlines use the country's modern and efficient airport as a connection point.

THAILAND

This kingdom enjoyed the world's highest economic growth rate between 1985 and 1995. During that period, expansion averaged nearly 9 percent per year. Growth slowed with the Asian economic downturn in the late 1990s, but Thailand's economy has rebounded strongly in the early twenty-first century. The country enjoys the benefits of a free-market economy and holds a positive attitude toward foreign investment. As a result, Thailand has been able to develop a modern economy that produces a variety of goods and services. It is a major producer of computers and electrical appliances and ranks as one of the three top producers of tungsten and tin. Other industries include textiles and garments, agricultural processing including beverages and tobacco, and light manufacturing. During recent decades, tourism has grown rapidly in importance, but this industry received a shocking setback with the devastation that resulted from the December 2004 tsunami that ravaged its shores.

Slightly more than 10 percent of the population is engaged in agriculture. Rice, cassava (tapioca), rubber, corn, sugarcane, coconuts, and soybeans are produced. Thailand has some oil reserves, but the country imports fuels and other raw materials for industrial use. Major trading partners include the United States, Japan, Singapore, China, and Malaysia. Air and water pollution are major challenges for the country, as is deforestation, which has depleted major portions of the country's tropical woodlands.

VIETNAM

The country suffers from a very high population density. This factor, combined with Communist leadership that is slow to move from a centrally controlled economy to a free-market system, has hampered Vietnam's growth. With increased connections to the outside world and more free-market opportunities, the economy's growth rate has increased in recent years. It still has a long way to go, however, as nearly 40 percent of the population is below the poverty level, 25 percent is unemployed, and nearly two-thirds of the work force is still engaged in agriculture.

Vietnam's trade is slowly increasing and has been boosted by a 2000 bilateral agreement with the United States that offers a promise of increasing exports. Present exports include crude oil, rice, coffee, rubber, tea, garments, and shoes. The country must import machinery and equipment, petroleum products, fertilizer, steel products, raw cotton, grain, and cement. The United States, Japan, Singapore, China, and South Korea are some of Vietnam's major trading partners.

This survey of the economies of Southeast Asia provides a brief picture of the pieces of this region's economic activity. Another major thread that ties this region together is provided by ASEAN. This organization has provided key economic ties among the ten countries in the region.

Farmers work the land along the city wall of Hue, Vietnam. Nearly 40 percent of the population is below the poverty level, 25 percent is unemployed, and nearly two-thirds of the work force is still engaged in agriculture.

SELECTED SOUTHEAST ASIAN ECONOMIC DATA (2004)

	GDP (PPP)	GDP by Sector	GDP Per Capita (PPP)	GDP Growth Rate	Labor Force	ASEAN Membership Starting Year	Currency
Brunei	$5.9 billion	n/a	$17,600	3%	Gov't 48% Ser. 42%	1984	Bruneian dollar
Burma	$70 billion	Ag. 60% Ind. 9% Ser. 31%	$1,660	3.3%	Ag. 70% Ind. 7% Ser. 23%	1997	kyat
Cambodia	$19.7 billion	Ag. 40% Ind. 20% Ser. 40%	$1,500	5.2%	Ag. 80%	1999	riel
Indonesia	$663 billion	Ag. 17% Ind. 41% Ser. 42%	$3,100	3.5%	Ag. 45% Ind. 16% Ser. 39%	1967	rupiah
Laos	$9.9 billion	Ag.53% Ind. 23% Ser. 24%	$1,700	5.5%	Ag. 80%	1997	kip
Malaysia	$210 billion	Ag. 12% Ind. 40% Ser. 48%	$9,300	4.2%	Ag. 16% Ind. 27% Ser. 48% Other 9%	1967	ringgit
Philippines	$356 billion	Ag. 15% Ind. 31% Ser. 54%	$4,200	4.6%	Ag. 39.8% Ind. 15.6% Ser. 37.1 Other 7.5%	1967	peso
Singapore	$105 billion	Ind. 33% Ser. 67%	$24,000	2.2%	Ind. 34% Ser. 35% Trans/Comm 9% Other 22%	1967	Singapore dollar
Thailand	$429 billion	Ag. 11% Ind. 40% Ser. 49%	$6,900	5.2%	Ag. 54% Ind. 15% Ser. 31%	1967	baht
Vietnam	$183 billion	Ag. 24% Ind. 37% Ser. 39%	$2,250	6%	Ag. 63% Ind. & Ser. 37%	1995	dong

Ag., Agriculture; Ind., Industry; PPP, purchasing power parity; Ser., Services; Trans/Comm, Transportation and Communications.

THE ASSOCIATION OF SOUTHEAST ASIAN NATIONS (ASEAN)

At the turn of the twenty-first century, United Nations Secretary-General Kofi Annan said, "Today, ASEAN is not only a well-functioning, indispensable reality in the region; it is a real force to be reckoned with far beyond the region." This statement reflects the remarkable transition of ASEAN from its humble roots in 1967 to its emergence as a worldwide force today. Before ASEAN, trade among member countries was negligible and most economies were tied to agriculture. People were often on subsistence living standards, with low average annual incomes.

Today, ASEAN has achieved remarkable success and has doubled its membership from the original five countries to the current membership of ten. The ASEAN declaration states that the aims and purposes of the Association are twofold:

1. To accelerate economic growth, social progress, and cultural development in the region through joint endeavors in the spirit of equality and partnership in order to strengthen the foundation for a prosperous and peaceful community of Southeast Asian nations
2. To promote regional peace and stability through abiding respect for justice and the rule of law in the relationship among countries in the region and adherence to the principles of the United Nations Charter

ASEAN has an annual meeting of the heads of the government; this group serves as the organization's decision-making body. Day-to-day activities are initiated and managed by the office of the secretary-general of ASEAN, who is appointed for a five-year term. ASEAN also has many working groups and committees, each of which is responsible for certain of the organization's efforts.

ASEAN is connected to the world. It attempts to advance relationships with other countries, particularly trade relationships.

Ministers pose for group pictures during the Press Conference of ASEAN + 3 Finance Ministers Meeting and Launch of AsianBondsOnline, May 15, 2004. Since its humble beginning in 1967, ASEAN has emerged as a worldwide force, building a stronger economy for all of Southeast Asia.

ASEAN holds annual meetings with important Asian trading nations including China, Japan, and South Korea, and also with others called dialog partners, such as the United States, Canada, Australia, India, and the European Union.

Within Southeast Asia, ASEAN is working to reduce trade barriers and to increase economic integration. Efforts to improve transportation and communication within the region, along with increasing tourism, are just a few of the plans included in ASEAN's Vision 2020, which was adopted in 1997. The organization also is working to ensure that the region is developed as a peaceful and stable nuclear-free zone.

The countries of Southeast Asia have been progressing at varying speeds since the end of World War II. The process of colonies turning into countries has often been difficult and fraught with problems. Hurdles to stable development include handicaps such as corruption, political instability, poverty, pollution, and lack of capital. Regional efforts such as ASEAN have helped countries create a more open environment for cooperation and free trade. With more than half a billion people, moderate GDP growth rates, and a variety of natural resources, Southeast Asia is poised to strengthen its position as a powerful economic force in the world arena.

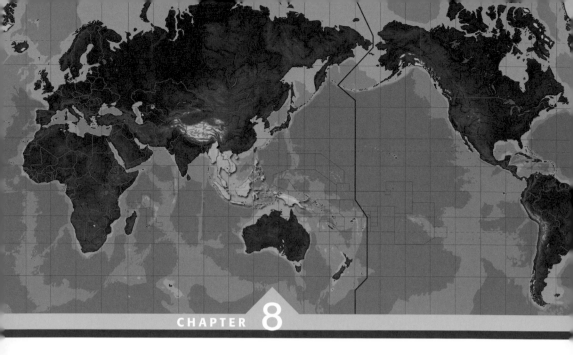

CHAPTER 8

Southeast Asia Looks Ahead

Thousands of colorful flags and political banners are waving on streets filled with people and cars honking horns. It's the city of Penang, Malaysia, and it is Sunday, March 21, 2004, national election day. *The New Sunday Times*'s headline boldly states, "Day of Decision." The election pits the moderate Barisan National (BN) party against a number of other parties including the rising Parti Islam SeMalaysia (PAS), and many people fear that a PAS victory will take the country on a less democratic route to a more extreme Islamic government. In 1999 elections, the PAS was the major winner in two states. The campaign was vigorously waged with high stakes for the country.

On April 5, 2004, another important election was conducted in Southeast Asia. This one was in Indonesia, the region's most populated country and one that has suffered attacks from al Qaeda–affiliated terrorists. Nearly a month later, in May, citizens and the world still waited to see if extremist Islamic parties had made gains in this vote that would help them gain control of the country's Legislative Branch. Some of these radical parties supported the violence of the Islamic terrorist groups. These elections were very important in demonstrating the patterns for Southeast Asia that were emerging from Malaysia and Indonesia.

Democracy has made significant inroads in Southeast Asia since World War II. Notable exceptions exist in Burma and Brunei, and change has been slow in Vietnam and Laos. Indonesia, Singapore, Malaysia, the Philippines, Cambodia, and Thailand, however, have made major steps forward to put more power in the hands of the people and the ballot box.

Economic advances have been remarkable during recent years in countries such as Singapore, Thailand, and Malaysia. Does the path of these countries point the way for other members of ASEAN? Forecasting the future can be a perilous practice. Perhaps the best way to consider the future of Southeast Asia is to look at historical trends and see how they are playing out today. These patterns may provide some clues that will help in anticipating what may take place in the future.

Political stability has increased significantly in the region in recent decades. There are no major wars taking place in the region today, and there has not been fighting in Indochina since the conflict in Cambodia ended in the late 1990s. This political stability is vital if all countries are to share in the economic opportunities in trade and development that can be fostered by ASEAN. Foreign investors are more apt to put capital to work in places like Vietnam, Indonesia, Cambodia, and the Philippines if the political and financial situations seem secure.

Although war is no longer a factor in Southeast Asia, terrorism has left its bloody footprints in some areas of the region. Indonesia, Thailand, and the Philippines have been touched by the terrorist acts of extremist Islamic or Christian groups. Most active in the region is Jemaah Islamiyah, which has connections to al Qaeda. If radical Islam captures more political influence, this will decrease political and economic stability and put public safety and economic growth at risk. Thus, elections in Indonesia and Malaysia are very important in gauging the impact of terrorism on the electorates and in the region.

The problem of corruption is huge in some Southeast Asian countries. It serves as a strong impediment to economic development: Money is skimmed off at many levels by people in both the public and private sectors. German-based Transparency International ranked 102 major countries in 2002 with its Corruption Perceptions Index (CPI). Among the countries in Southeast Asia, Singapore was ranked as the fifth least-corrupt country in the world, and Malaysia was a very respectable thirty-third. The Philippines, however, came in 77, Vietnam at 85, and Indonesia at an embarrassing 96; corruption is considered rampant in these three countries. (In comparison, Canada was ranked seventh and the United States sixteenth.) Thus, anticorruption efforts are vital in stabilizing the financial markets. Potential businesses and individuals are more inclined to invest if they know that their partners are honest. Singapore and Malaysia can serve as positive models with sound anticorruption business environments.

In the final examination, the people are the most important factor in securing a better future for themselves and their countries. Strong work habits, the elimination of ethnic and religious divisions, effective education systems, honesty, political participation, and other factors will help citizens strengthen their societies. All of these elements must be effectively addressed by the countries in the region.

With the people being key to successful governments, economies, and societies, some countries in the region are now embarking on efforts to strengthen the role and understanding of democratic citizenship. Indonesia, Malaysia, and

Thailand are conducting campaigns in civic education in which young people are prepared with programs like Project Citizen, a program that was developed by the Center for Civic Education in the United States. These programs are already playing a positive role in helping students understand their political structures and in developing public policies that will help improve their communities.

ASEAN continues to be a key player for improvement in the region. The organization has clearly demonstrated how it can serve as a positive institution of change in Southeast Asia as it works to shape a better future for member countries. This organization, which consists of all ten Southeast Asian nations, has developed a strategic plan for the future called Vision 2020. This plan was adopted by the member countries in Kuala Lumpur in 1997 and provides for a number of far-reaching collective goals for the region. One is that ASEAN will work to promote free trade and increase economic integration within the region. Other goals seek to improve the region's education, transportation, and communication systems and to promote food and energy security. The plan concludes by saying, "We pledge to our peoples our determination and commitment to bringing this ASEAN Vision for the Year 2020 into reality."

Obviously, there are many surprises that can affect the flow of events and development in Southeast Asia in the future. Perched on the Ring of Fire that coincides with the Pacific Rim, much of the region faces the constant threat of devastating earthquakes, tsunamis, and volcanic eruptions. These disruptions can cause loss of life and severe economic damage with the havoc they create. Human pollution and environmental degradation can also hamper progress. Fires in Indonesia in the late 1990s polluted the skies of most of Southeast Asia as the trade winds carried the dirty air to neighbors. Terrorism can also disrupt tourism, as shown by the bombings in Bali and Jakarta that were carried out by the evil hand of terrorists who sought to disrupt social harmony. Separatist movements in the Philippines,

Thailand, and Indonesia can also disrupt these societies. Thus, the trends and patterns that link the past, present, and future can be interrupted by many events, both natural and human. Without these interruptions, the course of Southeast Asia seems to be flowing in very positive directions.

What about the elections in Indonesia and Malaysia in 2004? The headline in the *New Strait Times* in Malaysia on Monday, March 22, 2004, read, "Landslide for BN." It was official: The moderates had decisively won the election. PAS, the more fundamental Islamic party, had been rejected on the national level and only gained seven seats in the parliament, whereas BN had won 198. PAS fell below the Chinese DAP party into a distant third place. At the same time, PAS lost one of the two states it controlled, which left it with only a two-vote majority in the state of Kelanatan.

The results of the legislative races in Indonesia were released on May 5, 2004. This election carried mixed results. The fundamentalist Islamic parties were rejected here as they had been in Malaysia. Two former generals, however, had risen to challenge the party in power—President Megawati Sukarnoputri's political party, the Indonesian Democratic Party of Struggle. The president's party took second place, and the party of Suharto, Indonesia's former military strongman, took first. Citizens seemed to vote for greater security because of the terrorist attacks that took place during President Sukarnoputri's term of office. Voters seemed to believe that the generals would take a stronger law-and-order stance.

What will be Southeast Asia's place in the future? Most likely, it will be closely intertwined with the United States and other Western countries and other Asian nations. In recent decades, many people from this region have migrated to the United States, Canada, and Western Europe. The economies are linked in thousands of ways that affect people daily. Continued development promises to connect Southeast Asia to the world by the sea and air. Technology has made this sprawling and fragmented region viable in the twenty-first century. It has enabled Southeast Asia to become a growing economic powerhouse and a strong political player on the world stage. The route to progress has always been a bit bumpy in this diverse and often turbulent region. Today, there are many positive trends that give strong indication of forward movement as the region builds connections to the rest of the world. Southeast Asia is no longer a remote spot "half a world away." Today, the region is our neighbor in the community of major world cultures.

Circa	
1,700,000 B.C.	Java man appears.
40,000 B.C.	Early inhabitants arrive in Indonesia and the Philippines from Malay Peninsula.
30,000 B.C.	Stone tools are used in the Philippines.
10,000 B.C.	Early Malaysian inhabitants, called the Negrito, use stone tools.
2500 B.C.	Pottery and stone tools used in Indonesia; Proto-Malays immigrate to Malaysian peninsula from China.
100 B.C.	Indians begin to arrive on the Malay Peninsula.
A.D. 100	Indian kingdoms begin to appear in Indonesia and on the Malay Peninsula.
425	Buddhism arrives in Sumatra.
600–1377	The Srivijaya Kingdom exists on Sumatra, Indonesia.
802–1431	The Khmer Empire exists in Cambodia.
825	Borobudur Temple is finished in Indonesia.
939–1883	The Vietnamese are independent.
1292	Marco Polo briefly stops in Sumatra and Java on his travel home.
Circa 1300	Islam is strongly entrenched on many of the islands of Indonesia.
Circa 1350	The Ayutthaya Kingdom (Kingdom of Siam) is established in Thailand.
1353–1707	The Lan Xang Kingdom exists in Laos.
1400	The port city of Malacca is founded on the Malay Peninsula.
1450	Malacca becomes the most important port in Southeast Asia; Islam arrives on the Malay Peninsula during this era of trade with the Middle East.
1511	The Portuguese arrive in Indonesia and the city of Malacca; Malacca's golden age ends.
1521	Magellan arrives in the Philippines and is killed by local warriors.
1560	The Spanish arrive at Manado in the Spice Islands.
1565–1898	The Philippines are a Spanish colony.
1579–1580	Englishman Sir Francis Drake visits various islands in Indonesia.
1596	The Dutch first arrive in Indonesia in four ships.
1602	The Dutch East India Company (VOC) is chartered in Indonesia.

1611	The British set up trading posts on various islands in Indonesia.
1641	The Dutch seize Malacca from the Portuguese.
1762	The British briefly capture Manila in the Philippines during the Seven Years' War.
1767	Ayutthaya is destroyed in a war with Burma.
1782	The Thai monarchy is restored with the Chakkri Dynasty in Bangkok.
1789	The British found a trading settlement in Penang, Malaysia.
1799	The Dutch East India Company goes bankrupt.
1811	Sir Thomas Stamford Raffles is appointed lieutenant governor of Java and Dependencies (Indonesia).
1811–1816	The British rule Java and Dependencies.
1816	Indonesia is returned to Dutch control by the British.
1819	Sir Thomas Stamford Raffles establishes a British trading post in Singapore.
1824	The Dutch turn over Malacca and Singapore to the British.
1859	The Dutch end slavery in the Netherlands Indies (Indonesia).
1874	Britain intervenes and forces conflicting Malay rulers to sign a peace treaty known as the Pangkor Agreement.
1887–1953	The French establish colonies in Indochina.
1893	Laos is added to French Indochina.
1898	Spain cedes the Philippines to the United States after the Spanish-American War.
1899	Emilio Aguinaldo proclaims the Malalos Constitution and the First Philippine Republic.
1899–1901	The Philippines wage war for independence from the United States.
1901–1934	The Philippines are a colony of the United States.
1909	The British control the entire Malay Peninsula.
1932	Siam (Thailand) establishes a constitutional monarchy.
1934	The Commonwealth of the Philippines is established.
1939	Siam's name is changed to Thailand.
1941–1945	Japan conquers Indonesia and the Philippines and occupies the colonies.

1942	Japan forces the British out of Malaya and Singapore; Siam declares war on the United States and United Kingdom.
1942–1945	Japan occupies Cambodia, Singapore, Malaya, and Burma.
1943	The Allies begin the retaking of Indonesia.
1945	Japan surrenders to the Allies; Sukarno declares Indonesia's independence from the Dutch; Indonesia's four-year war with Dutch begins, and a new constitution is implemented, with Sukarno declared president; the British regain control of Malaya.
1946	The Philippines gains independence; Manuel Roxas becomes first president.
1946–1954	The First Indochina War is waged.
1948	Burma gains independence.
1949	The Dutch relinquish control of Indonesia.
1950	Indonesia is admitted to the United Nations.
1953	Cambodia becomes independent.
1954	French rule in Vietnam ends; Vietnam divides into North Vietnam and South Vietnam; Laos becomes independent.
1955	Laos joins the United Nations.
1957	Federation of Malaya becomes independent.
1963	Sukarno is declared president for life in Indonesia; Malaysian Federation, which includes Singapore, is formed.
1964	The United States begins air strikes against North Vietnam.
1965	Indonesia withdraws from the United Nations; Singapore separates from the Malaysian Federation and becomes independent.
1965–1986	The Philippines is under Ferdinand Marcos's dictatorship.
1967	The Association of Southeast Asian Nations (ASEAN) is founded by Indonesia, Malaysia, Singapore, Thailand, and the Philippines; Indonesia rejoins the United Nations.
1970	Prince Norodom Sihanouk is removed, and the monarchy ends in U.S.-supported coup in Cambodia.
1975	South Vietnam collapses as Saigon falls; Communist Pathet Lao seizes control of the government of Laos; Khmer Rouge, led by Pol Pot, takes control in Cambodia, more than 3 million die in the ensuing violence.
1976	North Vietnam and South Vietnam unify.

1978	Vietnam invades Cambodia.
1979	Vietnamese-dominated People's Republic of Kampuchea is established in Cambodia; China launches an unsuccessful attack on Vietnam because of the situation in Cambodia under Pol Pot.
1984	Brunei becomes independent and joins ASEAN.
1986	Ferdinand Marcos is forced out of the Philippines and into exile; Corazon Aquino, widow of Marcos's murdered political opponent Benigno Aquino, is elected president of the Philippines.
1988	A border war between Laos and Thailand erupts.
1989	Burma's military government adopts the country name Myanmar; Vietnamese troops withdraw from Cambodia; Prince Sihanouk leads revolt against Khmer Rouge government forces.
1991	A peace agreement is signed in Cambodia, and the country is placed under UN supervision.
1992	The United States closes its last military bases in the Philippines.
1994	United States ends the 19-year trade embargo against Vietnam.
1995	Vietnam joins ASEAN; the United States and Vietnam establish full diplomatic relations; Laos, Cambodia, Thailand, and Vietnam form the Mekong River Commission.
1997	Burma and Laos join ASEAN.
1997–1998	Financial crises occur in Southeast Asia.
1998	The last Khmer Rouge forces surrender.
1999	Cambodia joins ASEAN.
2000	Vietnam and the United States sign a trade agreement.
2002	A Bali nightclub is bombed by terrorists affiliated with al Qaeda and more than 200 are killed.
2003	Jemaah Islamiyah bombs the Jakarta Marriott Hotel.
2004	Earthquake on ocean floor off Indonesian island of Sumatra on December 26 creates a tsunami that kills an estimated 250,000 people around the Indian Ocean basin, leaves millions homeless, and causes billions of dollars in damage.

Baker, Jim. *Crossroads: A Popular History of Malaysia & Singapore*. Singapore and Kuala Lampur: Times Books International, 1999.

Baxter, Craig, Yogendra K. Malik, Charles H. Kennedy, and Robert C. Oberst. *Government and Politics in South Asia*. Boulder, CO: Westview Press, 2001.

Chandler, David. *A History of Cambodia*. Boulder, CO: Westview Press, 2000.

Collins, Alan. *Security and Southeast Asia: Domestic, Regional, and Global Issues*. Boulder, CO: Lynne Rienner Publishers, 2003.

Cribb, Robert. *Historical Atlas of Indonesia*. Honolulu: University of Hawaii Press, 2000.

Daws, Gavan and Marty Fujita. *Archipelago: Islands of Indonesia*. Los Angeles: University of California Press, 1999.

Duiker, William J. *Vietnam: Revolution in Transition (Nations of the Modern World, Asia)*. Boulder, CO: Westview Press, 1995.

Gillespie, Carol Ann. *Bahrain (Modern World Nations)*. Philadelphia: Chelsea House Publishers, 2002.

Gupta, Avijit. *The Physical Geography of Southeast Asia (Oxford Regional Environments)*. Oxford: Oxford University Press, 2005.

Heidhues, Mary Somer. *Southeast Asia: A Concise History*. London: Thames & Hudson, 2001.

Higham, Charles. *Early Cultures of Mainland Southeast Asia*. Chicago: Art Media Resources, Ltd., 2003.

Jamieson, Neil L. *Understanding Vietnam*. Los Angeles: University of California Press, 1995.

Leinbach, Thomas R., and Richard Ulack. New York, *Southeast Asia: Diversity and Development*. New York: Prentice-Hall, 1999.

McCloud, Donald G. *Southeast Asia: Tradition and Modernity in the Contemporary World*. Boulder, CO: Westview Press, 1995.

Mildenstein, Tammy, and Samuel Cord Stier. *The Philippines (Modern World Nations)*. Philadelphia: Chelsea House Publishers, 2004.

Moreland, Martin, and Caroline Courtauld. *Burma (Myanmar)*. Hong Kong: Odyssey Publications, Ltd., 1998.

Nesadurai, Helen Sharmini. *Globalization, Domestic Politics and Regionalism: The ASEAN Free Trade Area*. London and New York: Routledge, 2003.

Owen, Norman G., David Chandler, and William R. Roff. *The Emergence of Modern Southeast Asia: A New History*. Honolulu: University of Hawaii Press, 2004.

Osborne, Milton. *Southeast Asia: An Introductory History*. New South Wales: Allen & Unwin Pty., 2001.

Parkes, Carl. *Southeast Asia (Moon Handbooks)*. Emeryville, California: Avelon Travel Publishing, 2001.

Phillips, Douglas A. *Indonesia (Modern World Nations)*. Philadelphia: Chelsea House Publishers, 2005.

Phillips, Douglas A., and Steven C. Levi. *The Pacific Rim Region: Emerging Giant*. Hillside, NJ: Enslow Publishers, Inc. 1988.

Rawson, Philip S. *The Art of Southeast Asia: Cambodia Vietnam Thailand Laos Burma Java Bali (World of Art)*. London: Thames & Hudson, 1990.

Raymer, Steve. *Living Faith: Inside the Muslim World of Southeast Asia*. Boston: Tuttle Publishing, 2002.

Rigg, Jonathon. *Southeast Asia: A Region in Transition: A Thematic Human Geography of the Asean Region*. New South Wales: Allen & Unwin Pty., 1991.

Sardesai, D.R. *Southeast Asia: Past & Present*. Boulder, CO: Westview Press, 2003.

Stuart-Fox, Martin. *A History of Laos*. Cambridge: Cambridge University Press, 1997.

Tarling, Nicholas. *The Cambridge History of Southeast Asia*. Cambridge: Cambridge University Press, 1999.

Tarling, Nicholas. *Nations and States in Southeast Asia*. Cambridge: Cambridge University Press, 1998.

Taylor, Jean Gelman. *Indonesia: Peoples and Histories*. New Haven and London: Yale University Press, 2003.

Weightman, Barbara A. *Dragons and Tigers: A Geography of South, East, and Southeast Asia, Updated Edition*. New York: John Wiley & Sons, 2004.

Wyatt, David K. *Thailand: A Short History*. New Haven: Yale University Press, 2003.

BOOKS

Abuza, Zachary. *Militant Islam in Southeast Asia: Crucible of Terror*. Boulder, CO: Lynne Rienner, 2003.

Alatas, Syed Farid, and Farid Alatas. *Democracy and Authoritarianism in Indonesia and Malaysia: The Rise of the Post-Colonial State*. New York: Palgrave Macmillan, 1997.

Anwar, Dewi Fortuna. *Indonesia in ASEAN: Foreign Policy and Regionalism*. New York: Palgrave Macmillan, 1994.

Acharya, Amitav. *Constructing a Security Community in Southeast Asia: ASEAN and the Problem of Regional Order*. London and New York: Routledge, 2001.

Baker, Jim. *Crossroads: A Popular History of Malaysia & Singapore*. Singapore: Times Books International, 1999.

Baxter, Craig, Yogendra K. Malik, Charles H. Kennedy, and Robert C. Oberst. *Government and Politics in South Asia*. Boulder, CO: Westview Press, 2001.

Chandler, David. *A History of Cambodia*. Boulder, CO: Westview Press, 2000.

Chandler, David P. *The Land and People of Cambodia. Portraits of the Nations*. New York: Harpercollins, 1991.

Collins, Alan. *Security and Southeast Asia: Domestic, Regional, and Global Issues*. Boulder, CO: Lynne Rienner, 2003.

Cribb, Robert. *Historical Atlas of Indonesia*. Honolulu: University of Hawaii Press, 2000.

Daws, Gavan, and Marty Fujita. *Archipelago: Islands of Indonesia*. Berkley: University of California Press, 1999.

Duiker, William J. *Vietnam: Revolution in Transition. Nations of the Modern World, Asia*. Boulder, CO: Westview Press, 1995.

Einfield, Jann (ed). *Indonesia. History of Nations*. Chicago: Greenhaven Press, 2004.

Gillespie, Carol Ann. *Bahrain (Modern World Nations)*. Philadelphia: Chelsea House Publishers, 2002.

Gouri, Mirpuri, and Robert Cooper. *Indonesia. Cultures of the World*. Salt Lake City, UT: Benchmark Books, 2001.

Gupta, Avijit. *The Physical Geography of Southeast Asia. Oxford Regional Environments.* Oxford: Oxford University Press, 2005.

Heidhues, Mary Somer. *Southeast Asia: A Concise History.* Thames & Hudson, 2001.

Higham, Charles. *Early Cultures of Mainland Southeast Asia.* Chicago: Art Media Resources, Ltd., 2003.

Jacobs, Judy. *Indonesia: A Nation of Islands. Discovering Our Heritage.* Minneapolis: Dillon Press, 1990.

Jamieson, Neil L. *Understanding Vietnam.* Berkley: University of California Press, 1995.

Leinbach, Thomas R., and Richard Ulack. *Southeast Asia: Diversity and Development.* New York: Prentice-Hall, 1999.

Lyle, Gary. *Indonesia.* Philadelphia: Chelsea House Publishers, 1998.

Major, John S. *The Land and People of Malaysia and Brunei. Portraits of the Nations.* New York: Harpercollins Childrens Books, 1991.

Martin, Fred. *Step into Indonesia.* Oxford: Heinemann Educational Books-Library Division, 1998.

McCloud, Donald G. *Southeast Asia: Tradition and Modernity in the Contemporary World.* Boulder, CO: Westview Press, 1995.

Mildenstein, Tammy, and Samuel Cord Stier. *The Philippines (Modern World Nations).* Philadelphia: Chelsea House Publishers, 2004.

Moreland, Martin, and Caroline Courtauld. *Burma (Myanmar),* Hong Kong: Odyssey Publications, Ltd., 1998.

Nesadurai, Helen Sharmini. *Globalization, Domestic Politics and Regionalism: The ASEAN Free Trade Area.* London and New York: Routledge, 2003.

Olesky, Walter G. *The Philippines. Enchantment of the World, Second Series.* New York: Children's Press, 2000.

Osborne, Milton. *Southeast Asia: An Introductory History.* Sydney, London, and Boston: Allen & Unwin Pty., Ltd, 2001.

Owen, Norman G., David Chandler, and William R. Roff. *The Emergence of Modern Southeast Asia: A New History.* Honolulu: University of Hawaii Press, 2004.

Phillips, Douglas A. *Indonesia (Modern World Nations).* Philadelphia: Chelsea House Publishers, 2005.

Phillips, Douglas A., and Steven C. Levi. *The Pacific Rim Region: Emerging Giant*. Berkley Heights, NJ: Enslow Publishers, Inc., 1988.

Rawson, Philip S. *The Art of Southeast Asia: Cambodia Vietnam Thailand Laos Burma Java Bali (World of Art)*. London: Thames and Hudson, 1990.

Raymer, Steve. *Living Faith: Inside the Muslim World of Southeast Asia*. Boston: Tuttle Publishing, 2002.

Ricklefs, M. C. *A History of Modern Indonesia Since C. 1200*. Stanford, CA: Stanford University Press, 2002.

Rigg, Jonathon. *Southeast Asia: A Region in Transition: A Thematic Human Geography of the ASEAN Region*. Sydney, London, and Boston: Allen & Unwin Pty., Ltd., 1991.

Sardesai, D. R. *Southeast Asia: Past & Present*. Boulder, CO: Westview Press, 2003.

Swearer, Donald K. *The Buddhist World of Southeast Asia (SUNY Series in Religion)*. Albany: State University of New York Press, 1995.

Steinburg, David I. *Burma: The State of Myanmar*. Washington: Georgetown University Press, 2002.

Stuart-Fox, Martin. *A History of Laos*. Cambridge: Cambridge University Press, 1997.

Tarling, Nicholas. *The Cambridge History of Southeast Asia*. Cambridge: Cambridge University Press, 1999.

Tarling, Nicholas. *Nations and States in Southeast Asia*. Cambridge: Cambridge University Press, 1998.

Taylor, Jean Gelman. *Indonesia: Peoples and Histories*. New Haven, CT: Yale University Press, 2003.

Warren, William, and Luca Invernizzi Tettoni. *Thailand: The Golden Kingdom*. Boston: Periplus Editions, 1999.

Weightman, Barbara A. *Dragons and Tigers: A Geography of South, East, and Southeast Asia, Updated Edition*. New York: John Wiley & Sons, 2004.

Wills, Karen. *Vietnam. Modern Nations of the World*. Chicago: Greenhaven Press, 2000.

Woods, Damon. *The Philippines: A Global Studies Handbook. Global Studies*. New York: ABC-CLIO, 2005.

Wyatt, David K. *Thailand: A Short History*. New Haven, CT: Yale University Press, 2003.

WEBSITES

About.com
http://geography.about.com/

This site provides an assortment of geographic information about Southeast Asia and other areas.

ASEAN Secretariat
http://www.aseansec.org/home.htm

This is the home page of the Association of Southeast Asian Nations (ASEAN).

Asia Society
http://www.asiasociety.org

This Web site features information about aspects of Asian culture and society.

Australian Asian Education Foundation
http://www.curriculum.edu.au/accessasia/

This site gives general information and curriculum resources on Thailand, Vietnam, and Indonesia.

CNN's Talk Asia
http://edition.cnn.com/ASIA/talkasia/

This site contains information about current events in Asia, combining articles from CNN, *Time,* and *Asiaweek.*

Country Reports
http://www.countryreports.org/

This site provides information on countries of the world.

Duke University Southeast Asian Resources
http://www.lib.duke.edu/ias/SEAsia/#internet

This site provides a variety of resources on Southeast Asia.

U.S. Library of Congress
http://lcweb2.loc.gov/frd/cs/cshome.html

This site provides extensive historic, geographic, economic, and other information on Asian and other world countries.

The World Factbook
http://www.cia.gov/cia/publications/factbook/

This Central Intelligence Agency (CIA) site provides up-to-date information about countries of the world.

page:

2: © Mapping Specialists, Ltd.
3: New Millennium Images
9: New Millennium Images
11: Associated Press, AP/Peter Dejong
14: Associated Press, AP/Emerito Antonio
17: © Mapping Specialists, Ltd.
21: © Sally A. Morgan; Ecoscene/CORBIS
23: New Millennium Images
28; © Chris Hellier/CORBIS
42: Associated Press, AP
44: Associated Press, AP
46: © Douglas A. Phillips
50: Associated Press, AP

54: New Millennium Images
56: © Mapping Specialists, Ltd.
64: © Douglas A. Phillips
67: New Millennium Images
74: Associated Press, AP/Vincent Thian
79: © Douglas A. Phillips
80: Associated Press, AP/Teh Eng Koon
88: Associated Press, AP/Andy Wong
89: © Mapping Specialists, Ltd.
97: © Steve Raymer/CORBIS
100: Associated Press, AP/Ahn Young-joon
Cover: © Catherine Karnow/CORBIS

DOUGLAS A. PHILLIPS is a lifetime educator, writer, and consultant who has worked and traveled in more than 85 countries on six continents. During his career, he has worked as a middle school teacher, a curriculum developer, an author, and a trainer of educators in many countries around the world. He has served as the president of the National Council for Geographic Education and has received the Outstanding Service Award from the National Council for the Social Studies, along with numerous other awards. He, his wife, and his two sons now reside in Arizona—a daughter is in Texas—where he writes and serves as an educational consultant for the Center for Civic Education. He has traveled widely in Southeast Asia and understands the importance of this region to the world today.

CHARLES F. ("FRITZ") GRITZNER is Distinguished Professor of Geography at South Dakota University in Brookings. He is now in his fifth decade of college teaching and research. During his career, he has taught more than 60 different courses, spanning the fields of physical, cultural, and regional geography. In addition to his teaching, he enjoys writing, working with teachers, and sharing his love for geography with students. As consulting editor for the MODERN WORLD NATIONS series, he has a wonderful opportunity to combine each of these "hobbies." Fritz has served as both President and Executive Director of the National Council for Geographic Education and has received the Council's highest honor, the George J. Miller Award for Distinguished Service. In March 2004, he won the Distinguished Teaching award from the American Association of Geographers at their annual meeting held in Philadelphia.